ARSENAL 101

A POCKET GUIDE IN 101 MOMENTS, FACTS, CHARACTERS AND GAMES

RAB MACWILLIAM

POLARIS
PUBLISHING

This edition first published in 2021 by

POLARIS PUBLISHING LTD
c/o Aberdein Considine
2nd Floor, Elder House
Multrees Walk
Edinburgh, EH1 3DX

Distributed by
Birlinn Limited

www.polarispublishing.com

ISBN: 9781913538149
eBook ISBN: 9781913538064

THIS IS AN UNOFFICIAL PRODUCT

British Library Cataloguing-in-Publication Data
A catalogue record for this book is available on request from the British Library.

Designed and typeset by Polaris Publishing, Edinburgh
Printed in Great Britain by MBM Print SCS Limited, East Kilbride

INTRODUCTION

As you gaze idly eastward out the window of your train passing through suburban north London on its way to King's Cross St Pancras, it's difficult to miss what appears to be a large amphitheatre towering over the area.

This imposing structure, stretching over 17 acres of prime inner-city land, is the Emirates Stadium, which since 2006 has been home to one of the world's most famous sporting institutions: Arsenal Football Club.

The stadium rises imperiously over this busy part of north London which includes Finsbury Park, Holloway, Islington and other neighbouring areas. This new complex also overlooks, only a few hundred yards from its entrance, the site of the old Highbury Stadium, Arsenal's home from 1913 until its move to the grander premises.

Prior to Highbury, the club based itself in Woolwich, ten miles to the south across the River Thames, and that is where this book begins the fascinating story of Arsenal Football Club.

*

The club was founded in 1886 by a group of football-loving workmen at Woolwich Arsenal. Its nomadic early existence – from

Plumstead Common, via Manor Ground, Invicta Ground, back to Manor Ground and, in 1913, to Highbury – was mirrored in its change of name from Dial Square, Royal Arsenal, Woolwich Arsenal, The Arsenal and finally Arsenal, the name on which it settled after it reached Highbury.

Arsenal's first legendary period was during the 1930s when, under the formative, charismatic leadership of manager Herbert Chapman, they won five League titles and two FA Cups. After World War Two, Arsenal's status in English football became less dominant, but from the mid-1960s under manager Bertie Mee and trainer Don Howe, the club captured the Inter-Cities Fairs Cup, followed by, in 1970/71, the double of League title and FA Cup.

Arsenal again won the FA Cup in 1979 with manager Terry Neill, but it was the return as manager in 1986 of ex-player George Graham which began to revitalise the club. When Graham departed in 1995, he had managed Arsenal to two League titles, two League Cups, an FA Cup and the European Cup-Winners' Cup.

The arrival in 1996 of Arsene Wenger, however, initiated a profound change in the club's culture, and Wenger oversaw Arsenal's second legendary period. During his 22 years in charge, Arsenal won two more Doubles, dominated English football with the 'Invincibles', moved to the Emirates, gained a further League title and five more FA Cups, and reached the Final of the Champions League. He left the club in 2018, and new manager Mikel Arteta, who took over after the brief tenure of Unai Emery, won the FA Cup in 2019/20, his first year in the role.

The Covid-19 pandemic played havoc with football clubs, crowd attendances and League fixtures worldwide in 2020/21, and Arsenal were no exception to the pandemic's impact. They endured an unhappy season, finishing in mid-table and defeated by Villarreal in the semi-final of the European League. But, as ever with Arsenal, they will soon be back and competing at the highest levels of the game.

*

This short description obviously does not reveal anything like the full story of Arsenal (including, for instance, that they are the only club in English football history never to have been relegated from the top division).

In the pages of this book, I hope that you, as an Arsenal supporter, a general football fan or an interested reader – perhaps all three – will discover much about the history of Arsenal which will inform, surprise and entertain you.

In keeping with the other titles in this series, I have selected, on a largely chronological basis, 101 aspects of the major events in this occasionally frustrating but always engaging and intriguing football club. *Arsenal 101* considers the club's history, from the early days on the Isle of Dogs where Arsenal played its first-ever game in 1886, to the close of the 2020/21 season at the Emirates.

The relative brevity of the book is deliberately designed to eliminate unnecessary detail and to concentrate on the essence of the story. *Arsenal 101* captures Arsenal's important, interesting and most memorable moments, games, competitions and remarkable incidents; it covers the entertaining and amusing events, origins of nicknames ('Gooners') and chants, people of influence, Arsenal fans, special events at Highbury, and relations with other English (particularly Spurs) and European clubs; and the changing impact on Arsenal of the younger players and the benefits (and otherwise) of the transfer market.

Last, but certainly by no means least, it discusses the managers and the special players – from Alex James and Cliff Bastin to Dennis Bergkamp and Cesc Fabregas – as well as the perhaps less gifted team members, all of whom have excelled in their attempts to ensure that Arsenal has been and remains an unpredictable but special and much-loved football club.

Rab MacWilliam
May 2021

1

Where it all kicked off

At the end of the 19th century, Woolwich was a fairly nondescript town in Kent lying to the south-east of London on the south bank of the River Thames.

Despite, or perhaps because of, the town's relative anonymity, it was home to Woolwich Arsenal, one of the country's largest suppliers of military weaponry and munitions to the soldiery and artillery of the far-flung British Empire.

As that century drew to a close, in the south-east of the country the 'gentlemen's sports' of cricket and rugby were the prevailing leisure activities, but the relatively new game of association football was quickly catching up. In the Midlands, northern England and Scotland the game was also rapidly gaining in popularity. Woolwich Arsenal hired workers from across the country.

In 1886 two artisans named Fred Beardsley and Morris Bates, from the ordnance works at Nottingham, arrived at Woolwich and met with Kirkcaldy-born David Danskin. Both newcomers had played for one of the leading clubs of the period, Nottingham Forest, while Danskin and several of his co-workers shared their fascination for the game and had been considering the idea of setting up a football club at the Arsenal.

Danskin organised a 15-man whip-round, bought a ball from the proceeds, and the fledgling players, needing a name for the team, settled on **Dial Square**, one of the Arsenal workshops.

Dial Square had been established in 1717 as the Arsenal's main canonry workshop (a fact which contributed to the club's later nickname of 'the Gunners').

Left-back and team captain Danskin was the first but certainly not the last Scotsman to influence the club's history. Along with fellow workmate Jack Humble, he organised the team's first game, which was played on marshy ground – lacking crossbars and pitch markings, and located alongside an open sewer – across the Thames on the Isle of Dogs, better known today as the location of Canary Wharf.

On 11 December 1886, these Dial Square players crossed the river on the long-established Woolwich Ferry, made their way to the Island, and defeated Eastern Wanderers 6-0. Enthused by their victory, the players met again two weeks later on Christmas Day at the Royal Oak public house in Plumstead, near to the Arsenal, and began to make plans.

2

Plumstead welcomes royalty

The players decided on a new name for the team and, combining a mention for their local pub with a rather ambitious flourish, they opted for **Royal Arsenal**. As they needed their own home pitch, they chose the run-down but adjacent Plumstead Common. Finally, in the interests of team cohesion, they required a unified strip. Beardsley contacted his old club, and Nottingham Forest obliged with the loan of all-red shirts (the white sleeves were adopted in the early 1930s) and a ball. 'The Reds', as they soon became known, then wasted little time in demonstrating their footballing credentials.

The team's first game as Royal Arsenal was a 6-1 victory over local rivals Erith on 8 January 1887 at Plumstead Common. The Reds won seven matches that season, losing two. The following season Royal Arsenal played 24 games and won 14. One of their defeats, by a 2-1 margin, was on north London's Tottenham Marshes on 19 November 1887 against Tottenham Hotspur, the first encounter in what was to become an enduring rivalry.

By season 1889/90 Royal Arsenal's prowess on the pitch had earned them the soubriquet of 'Football Champions of the South', having established their supremacy over such London clubs as Tottenham, Millwall, Fulham, QPR and Clapton Orient.

That season the Reds won three cups which included the London Charity Cup at The Oval, beating Old Westminsters

3-1 in the Final, a game which was watched by over 10,000 spectators. They were, however, defeated 5-1 at home by the Swifts, one of the oldest and most experienced southern clubs, in the fourth and final preliminary round of the FA Cup, a national knock-out competition organised almost 20 years previously.

The Royal Arsenal team for the 1888/89 season. *Alamy*

3

On the road again

By now Royal Arsenal had outgrown the limitations of Plumstead Common. In 1888 they moved to the Manor Ground, where military wagons acted as grandstands, and by 1890 the club's home was the Invicta Ground ('Invicta' being Kent's motto), still close to the Arsenal but with a significantly increased capacity.

The club remained at Invicta for the following two seasons, where they attracted a crowd of over 12,000 for a friendly against Scottish champions Hearts and where they were building a sizeable local support: the *Guardian* noted that 'the Royal Arsenal was not without a considerable and confident following'.

The club's early success prompted the Invicta ground's owner to suggest a substantial rent increase, but this was rejected by the Reds. So, the start of season 1893/94 found the club back at the Manor Ground, opposite Plumstead station, where they were to remain for the following 20 years.

4

London's first professional club

The club's 1891 AGM at the Windsor Castle Music Hall was critical to the club's future. Professionalism had grudgingly been legalised by the FA in 1885, and the Football League, with associated professionalism, came into being from season 1888/89. The League, however, was entirely composed of northern clubs as the London FA abhorred the very idea of being paid to play football.

Royal Arsenal were becoming increasingly wary of northern clubs' incursions into their territory in order to nab their top players. At this meeting, therefore, it was decided that the club had to turn professional to prevent these attempted seductions and to gain financial viability.

Predictably, the London FA were furious at such ungentlemanly conduct, banned the club from all their competitions and expelled Royal Arsenal. For the following two seasons, Arsenal's on-pitch opposition consisted either of friendlies against non-London-based teams or of competing in the FA Cup, where they were routinely eliminated in the qualifying rounds.

The club's attempt in 1892 to establish a southern version of the Football League was welcomed by many of London's other clubs, but the proposal crumbled in the face of the London FA's obdurate refusal to agree. Nevertheless, Royal Arsenal pressed ahead with their expansionist plans, forming in 1893 a limited company to secure funding for the purchase of the Manor Ground. 'Royal' seemed an inappropriate, and perhaps impertinent, title for the club's new financial status, and the club's name was changed to **Woolwich Arsenal**.

That same year – 1893 – saw a potentially momentous upturn in the club's footballing and financial projections, the source for this unexpected reversal of fortune being the Football League.

5

Arsenal join the Football League

The English Football League was inspired by (yes, another) Scotsman, a director of Aston Villa, William McGregor. The League contained 12 professional clubs from the north and Midlands, and played its opening season in 1888/89.

From the start of season 1893/94 the League increased its Second Division from 12 to 15 clubs. Two First Division clubs haughtily refused relegation and quit, while two others were promoted, leaving space for five new entrants. Arsenal applied, were accepted and became the first southern club to join the League. Indeed, the potential for this move had been one of the main factors underlying the club's recent financial activities.

The first game in their so-far brief but rapidly escalating career was at the revamped Manor Ground on 2 September 1893 against Newcastle United. With 10,000 spectators present, Woolwich Arsenal drew 2-2, with William Shaw scoring the club's first-ever League goal, an encouraging result for the London side on this historic occasion.

6

Life in the Second Division

As the only southern club in the League, Woolwich Arsenal faced unreliable travel and substandard accommodation problems during their 11-year run in the lower division. As the club remained financially shaky, they also suffered from other League clubs enticing away several of their better players.

Nonetheless, they normally finished in or around mid-table at season's end, with most of their victories at home and their arduous away trips ending in defeat. Season 1896/97 was their worst season, when they crashed to a record 8-0 League defeat at Loughborough Town, were eliminated from the FA Cup by lowly Southern League Millwall and finished tenth in the League.

Manager-less until now, they appointed two managers in quick succession and this helped their performances on the pitch (including a 12-0 revenge defeat of Loughborough Town, a result which still today remains their record score). However, from 1900/01 a new manager was to make a significant difference.

7

Arsenal's first international player

At the start of the 1895/96 season, Woolwich Arsenal were joined by a quality centre-half, a position which, in those days, was a midfield one. Caesar Llewellyn Jenkyns was born in Wales (well, where else?) and looked every inch the aristocrat, from his proud demeanour to his luxuriant, waxed moustache.

He arrived from Small Heath, today's Birmingham City, but his record belied his physical impression, as he had been sent off on at least four occasions, at a time when marching orders were extremely rare in the game, and he had assaulted remonstrating spectators. This tough and clearly determined player stayed with the club for only one season, during which, on 21 March 1896, he became the first Arsenal player to achieve international recognition when he was capped for his country in a game against Scotland.

He left at the season's end for Newton Heath (Manchester United) and eventually retired to join the police force, a not inappropriate career decision, but his name endures in Arsenal's history.

8

Bradshaw's boys done well

The appointment in 1900 of Harry Bradshaw (again, a Scotsman) as manager gave renewed impetus to the club, who were losing players to the Boer War effort and who remained financially troubled.

Under Bradshaw's stewardship, Woolwich Arsenal strengthened their defence while also adopting speedy movement and inventive, quick passing, due mainly to the majority of the team being Scottish. This 'passing game' was Scotland's contribution to football, and Bradshaw's astute selection and man-management skills encouraged its full deployment on the pitch. An early indication of the manager's methods was that, in his first season of 1900/01, his team beat Blackburn Rovers in the FA Cup, thereby reaching the second round of the competition and also defeating a First Division side, both for the first time.

During Bradshaw's four-year tenure, as the club rose up the Second Division, so also did gates increase. As an example, in February 1903 a record home crowd of over 24,000 watched an FA Cup tie against Sheffield United. The following season – 1903/04 – Woolwich Arsenal were unbeaten at home all season, scoring 65 home goals and conceding only five, and they finished the campaign one point behind leaders Preston North End. Along with Preston, they were promoted to the First Division.

An obscure, local works team only 20 years previously, Woolwich Arsenal were now at the pinnacle of the English game.

Harry Bradshaw.

9

Mixed fortunes

After his success, Bradshaw moved to Fulham, and Hibs ex-boss Phil Kelso took over as club manager. Kelso's player acquisitions were sensible choices: Charlie Sattenthwaite scored Arsenal's first top division goal in the 2-0 win over Wolves in September 1904/05, while keeper Jimmy Ashcroft became the first Arsenal player to win an England cap.

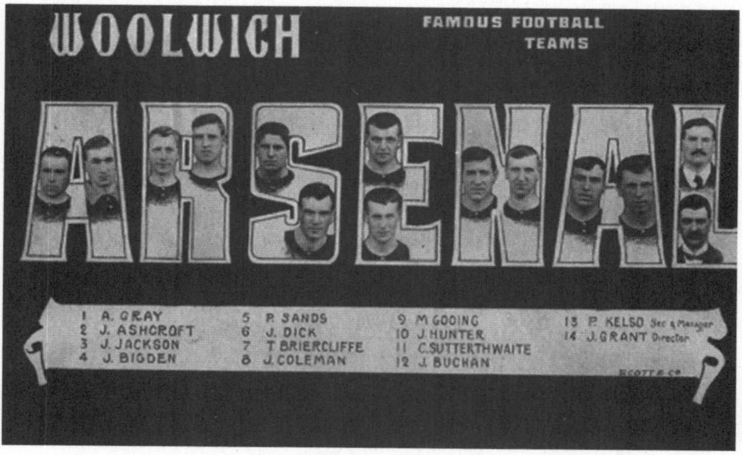

A postcard of the 1904/05 team.

Kelso also secured two successive FA Cup semi-finals in 1906 and 1907, losing both, but such dizzy heights had never before been achieved at the club. He also kept Woolwich Arsenal more or less in mid-table before he left in 1908, leaving his successor George Morrell (this time from Morton) to deal with another looming financial crisis.

The problems were linked, and were caused by slumping attendances at home, due partly to Plumstead's geographical location on London's extreme suburban edge, and also by the increasing competition for players and spectators from the new London clubs who were more centrally placed for public transport in the city.

Morrell stayed the course but was fortunate to escape relegation at the end of 1909/10. Things picked up slightly over the following two seasons, but at the end of 1912/13, with demoralised players, crowds having halved in number over five years, only three wins and 26 goals scored, and a League record low of 18 points, Woolwich Arsenal ended in bottom place and were relegated to the Second Division.

The club was technically bankrupt and supposedly had less than £20 in the bank. A saviour, however, had been working hard behind the scenes. Step forward, Henry Norris, and lead us on the road to Highbury Stadium and glory.

10

Mr Norris changes . . . everything

Henry Norris was a self-made man, a wealthy property developer and chairman of London's oldest club, Fulham FC. A headstrong, irascible and frequently ruthless individual, who could be charming when the situation required, he had bought Woolwich Arsenal in 1910 and he was determined to turn round the club's fortunes. His energetic scheming and, particularly, his financial investments undoubtedly saved the club from liquidation.

Norris and his Fulham co-director William Hall were convinced that Plumstead was too remote for a club which demonstrated Woolwich's potential. Norris first attempted to merge the club with Fulham, to no avail, and then suggested a ground-sharing scheme at Craven Cottage, with a similar lack of success. While Woolwich Arsenal were heading towards relegation, these two men were scouring sites around London in search of an appropriate, more central location for the club.

Eventually, they discovered a piece of land, owned by the Ecclesiastical Commission and used for sporting activities by St John's College of Divinity, which was close to public transport to and from central London, had a sizeable catchment area and was affordable. After several months of negotiation, Norris and the Commission agreed on a payment of £20,000 for a 21-year lease for a six-acre site which, from season 2013/14, would be Woolwich Arsenal's new home. The final deed of transfer was awarded divine approval by the signature of the Archbishop of Canterbury.

The club would, however, have to drop 'Woolwich' from their name, as the ground was located more than ten miles over the Thames in north London's Highbury. So, they were renamed 'The Arsenal', and twelve years later they formally became **Arsenal**, although today many fans still refer to 'the Arsenal'.

There was a good deal of work to be done on the site before it was ready for the start of season 1913/14. Undaunted, Norris and his builders set to work on the ground which was to be Arsenal's home for almost the next hundred years.

Henry Norris. *Colorsport*

11

Why Highbury?

There were, of course, objections to the sudden arrival of a football stadium in this relatively sedate neighbourhood, stemming from two main sources: local residents and other football clubs.

Many residents complained to the press and Islington Council, using such phrases as 'utter ruin' of the neighbourhood, as well as voicing concern at the stadium's impact on the valuation of local properties. These protesting voices did not include local shopkeepers and tradesmen. The council attempted to change St John's mind but the college refused to reconsider the deal.

The other principal objectors were Tottenham Hotspur and Clapton Orient whose grounds then were each situated within four miles of Highbury, were both competing Football League clubs and were concerned at the financial impact of Arsenal's arrival on their territories. A Football League special meeting in March 1913 listened to the clubs' complaints and concluded that the League had 'no right to interfere' with Arsenal's decision.

The new stadium, therefore, may have been unpopular in some quarters, but it was here to stay and the work continued on its completion. Norris embarked on a spending spree over that summer to ensure the ground would be in a fit state for the coming season. Using mud and earth from the newly constructed Piccadilly Line underground at nearby Gillespie Road station, Arsenal built terraces on three sides of the ground; they levelled the pitch by raising the north end by 11 feet and reducing the south by five feet; Archibald Leitch (no less) was commissioned to erect a grandstand; and a good deal more expense was incurred. Norris invested the staggering sum of £125,000 into the development of Highbury Stadium that summer.

Still in the Second Division, Arsenal missed promotion to the First by 0.09% of a goal in their first season at Highbury. War was declared against Germany on 4 August 1914 but the Football League played all of season 1914/15. With players and spectators increasingly joining the war effort, serious competitive football soon became a charade, and the League thereafter discontinued the competition until season 1919/20, nine months after hostilities had ceased.

Arsenal finished fifth in the Second Division in 1914/15, George Morrell was sacked as manager and, most importantly in the light of immediate post-war events, chairman Norris was owed a substantial sum of money. The only way he could realise this was by moving up to the First Division, which is exactly what he did.

12

First game at Highbury

Although the stadium was far from ready, and workmen and contractors' lorries were milling around, a decent-sized crowd of more than 20,000 turned up for the opening game of 1913/14 at the new Highbury ground. By contrast, Arsenal's final game at the Manor Ground in April of that year had attracted a mere 3,000.

Leicester Fosse, shortly to become Leicester City, were the opposition on 6 September and were beaten 2-1 by Arsenal, with the first Arsenal goal at Highbury coming from the head of centre-forward George Jobey, newly acquired from Newcastle United. In the second half, Jobey badly sprained an ankle, creating another moment of history when he became the first player ever to be stretchered off at the stadium.

As the Highbury dressing room was still being built, the club trainer borrowed a powered milk cart from the Gillespie Road milkman and drove the incapacitated Jobey back to his nearby digs, a somewhat ignoble end to the player's record-setting day. Jobey stayed with Arsenal till that season's end and then moved to Bradford Park Avenue, which did possess a functioning dressing room.

13

How did Norris manage it?

One of Arsenal's proudest claims – and there are plenty – is that they remain the only English League club never to have been relegated from the top division. However, others – principally Spurs fans – assert that, if Arsenal hadn't 'sneaked' their way into the First Division when and in the manner in which they did, they may never have reached the top league in the first place.

In *The Official Illustrated History Of Arsenal*, the authors make the atypically hyperbolic comment that, in 1919, 'Norris set out on the single most outrageous enterprise ever to be conceived in the history of English football'. What happened to cause the furore which created such an enduringly bitter rivalry between these two London clubs?

It began when the League announced that, from the start of season 1919/20, the post-war First Division would be increased from 20 to 22 clubs. Normally, this would ensure the survival of the First Division's bottom two clubs in 1914/15 – Chelsea and Tottenham Hotspur – and the promotion of the two leading Second Division sides – Derby County and Preston North End. However, this is not exactly what happened.

Sir Henry Norris (knighted in 1917 and elected a Tory MP in 1919), a born Machiavellian, spotted his opportunity. During the eight-month period between the end of the war and the English League's AGM in mid-1919, Norris used his newly enhanced status and his undeniably persuasive skills to campaign for Arsenal's promotion to the First Division. Dropping hints about possible pre-war match-fixing, cajoling and flattering his friends in other clubs, granting and seeking the return of favours and, no doubt, adopting a liberal attitude to his fund of cash, Norris was in his element.

At the AGM, Norris's close friend and League chairman 'Honest' John McKenna announced, as expected, that Derby and Preston would be promoted. Chelsea, perceived victims of mild chicanery in the pre-war final season, were also allowed to remain in the upper league. This left one place in the First Division. When McKenna then stated that Arsenal should be considered for promotion, all hell broke loose.

McKenna justified his reasoning on the grounds of Arsenal's longevity in the League (15 years longer than Tottenham) and the modern style and image which the club would bring to the League, particularly with the imposing new Highbury stadium (Tottenham had recently spent £50,000 on White Hart Lane, while Wolves – one place above Arsenal in 1914/15 – had joined the League four years before Arsenal). Third-placed Barnsley were equally furious.

A vote was then taken among the members. Arsenal received 18 votes, Tottenham eight and Wolves only four. Astonishingly – and leapfrogging three higher-placed clubs – Arsenal were in the First Division for season 1919/20.

There may well have been reasons other than Sir Henry's seemingly unscrupulous dealings behind the scenes, but these were not revealed nor have they ever been. Henry Norris's investments seemed to have been worthwhile, at least for him and Arsenal, but the deep enmity with Spurs can mainly be traced back to Norris's opportunistic gambles, and Arsenal would never be allowed to forget it.

14

Norris calls on Knighton

In early summer 1919 Norris appointed Leslie Knighton as manager although, as Knighton soon discovered, Norris continued to call the shots.

Norris stipulated that Knighton could pay only up to £1,000 on new players (the average transfer fee in the top league was £3,000), the player could not be smaller than 5 feet 8 inches, and the scouting system was to be scrapped. The new manager was resourceful and persuasive, however, and he enticed several quality players to Highbury. These included Tom Whittaker (a future trainer and manager at the club), Bob John, a half-back who stayed with Arsenal until 1937 and Billy Milne who became the club trainer in 1947. The long-serving Joe Shaw remained captain.

Knighton's first couple of seasons – 1919/20 and 1920/21 – were, given Norris's constraints, respectable ones for the club, ending in ninth and tenth place in the League. His second season also witnessed the first ever north London derby at Highbury, in front of a record 60,000 crowd and resulted in a 3-2 victory over Tottenham Hotspur. Thereafter, results went downhill for Arsenal. Aside from 11th place at the end of 1922/23, the other three seasons of Knighton's tenure found the club ending no higher than 17th.

The FA Cup was no better. In Knighton's six seasons as boss, Arsenal fluctuated between the embarrassing nadir of the 1921 first round 2-0 away defeat by Third Division QPR and the sunlit uplands of the 1922 quarter-final which, after their dismissal by Preston, was as far as they reached in the competition.

1920/21 full squad.

Back (left to right): T. Ratcliffe (Assistant trainer), James McEwen (Assistant Manager), Christopher Sebastian (Chris) Buckley, Francis Cownley, H. John Peters (Secretary), Jim Smith, Charlie Lewis, John 'Jack' Peart, Arthur Kempton, Stephen Dunn, E. Wood, Joe North, D.J. Plumb, Harold Adrian Walden.

Second row: G. Hardy (trainer), Henry Albert (Bert) White, William Naismith (Billy) Blyth, William Hall (Director), Sir Henry Norris (Chairman), John Wilkinson 'Jack' Humble (Director), Charles Doland Crisp (Director), George Wyatt Peachey (Director), Alf Jewett, John Dennis 'Jack' Butler, George Charlton Pattison, Leslie Knighton (Manager).

Sitting: Alex Graham, Alf Baker, Ernest Clark 'Tim' Williamson, Frank Bradshaw, Jock Rutherford, Joe Shaw, Arthur Hutchins, Fred Pagnam, Angus McKinnon.

Sitting on ground: Jimmy Hopkins, Clem Voysey, Arthur Rosbotham, Stephen B Rose, Freddie Groves, David Greenaway, Daniel 'Dick' Burgess, Joe Toner, Tom Whittaker, Walter Ernest Coopland. *Colorsport*

15

'A flock of lively lions'

Arsenal were drawn against West Ham away in the first round of the 1925 FA Cup, to be held in January. With their poor record in the competition and their continuing general underperformance, Arsenal were the underdogs. So when Knighton was approached by an Arsenal-supporting, Harley Street doctor and was offered 'courage pills' (almost certainly an amphetamine of some sort) to give to the players before kick-off, the manager was intrigued.

Having been assured of their legality, Knighton handed them out but the game was abandoned due to fog. The following Monday, the pills were dispensed, but the game was again fog-abandoned. Knighton had also taken a pill and, like his players, didn't care for the edginess and thirst of the after-effects. The third match went ahead, along with the pills and, although Arsenal rampaged all over West Ham, the score stayed 0-0. Knighton remarked that getting the team back to Highbury 'was like trying to drive a flock of lively lions'.

For the third replay the team refused the pills, settled down a bit and drew 2-2, both scored by Jimmy Brain. The final, pill-free replay saw the Hammers proceed 1-0 to round two, and the Arsenal 'speedfreaks' yet again out of the tournament.

This 'drug-assisted' policy was soon discarded, along with Knighton who was sacked towards the end of that season by a trophy-starved chairman. Knighton had done what he could with

Arsenal but he had suffered from Norris's constant interference and controlling nature. Knighton's subsequent career with such clubs as Birmingham and Chelsea demonstrated the high quality of his managerial ability.

However, Norris had that year bought the Highbury lease outright for £64,000, and Arsenal now owned the stadium. Finishing the season in 20th place – one spot above relegation – as well as the FA Cup debacle, did not augur well for the future of Norris's investment in the club.

Knighton claimed that his dismissal was provoked by Norris's unwillingness to pay him the £4,000 he was owed for a forthcoming benefit match. Although there may have been some truth to Knighton's allegation, Norris needed a new manager to turn around the club's fortunes and he knew just the man for the job.

16

A footballing revolution begins

Norris placed a prominent advertisement in the 11 May 1925 edition of the Manchester-based, weekly magazine *Athletic News*. It read as follows:

'Arsenal Football Club is open to receive applications for the position of Team Manager. He must be experienced and possess the highest qualifications for the post, both as to ability and personal character. Gentlemen whose sole ability to build up a good side depends on the payment of heavy and exorbitant transfer fees need not apply.'

The wording was designed to stress the elevated position of the club in the world of football, as well as to reinforce Norris's frugal yet canny attitude to the game. The ad was also superfluous, as the previous month he had sounded out – and the job had been accepted by – the very man Norris wanted.

Herbert Chapman joined Arsenal at the end of May. Over the following ten seasons, Chapman became regarded as one of the finest managers in the history of football. He is also considered by many as the inventor of the modern game.

17

Chapman takes over

A stocky Yorkshireman, Chapman developed his perceptive managerial skills while in charge of Northampton Town (where he had presciently mused 'a team can attack for too long'), Leeds City and, since 1921, Huddersfield Town.

With Huddersfield he had won their first (and only) FA Cup in 1922 and, soon after Chapman came to Highbury, the club had won their second successive First Division title. The third was to come the following year, aided by his use of swift counter-attacking, and by a 'stopper' centre-half to keep a close eye on the opposing centre-forward.

Norris was impressed by Chapman's record and agreed to his high salary (£2,000 per annum). For his part, the new manager saw in the club, its new stadium and its hinterland an arena where he could develop his football philosophy. The chairman accepted Chapman's assessment that it would take five years to assemble an Arsenal team capable of winning a trophy. Norris, however, would not be present for the celebration, as he was to be permanently suspended by the FA in 1929 for supposed financial shenanigans, and the Hill-Wood dynasty, less involved than was Norris in on-pitch matters, were to take over.

Opposite: Herbert Chapman. *Alamy*

18

'Offside already?'

Over the years, the 'offside trap' had been perfected by various First Division defences. Perhaps the most notorious was at Newcastle United, at whose railway station the above observation was made by a visiting club's forward on hearing the stationmaster's whistle.

Since the 1860s the laws of football had required at least three defenders to be between their goal and the attacking opposition, or the offending forward was ruled offside. This was now being seen as leading to a declining number of goals, constant stoppages in play, boring matches and dwindling crowds. Eventually, the FA agreed. From season 1925/26, the number of defenders was reduced from three to two.

This change in the laws of football was described as 'the crack of a shot that started an avalanche'. Suddenly, forwards had more space, longer passes were possible and goals were easier to score. Indeed, this was the principal reason that some observers opposed the change, claiming that it gave attacking players an unfair advantage.

In the opening match of the new season Aston Villa scored ten goals against Burnley, and the crowds started returning to the stadiums.

19

Chapman's opening seasons

Chapman's first signing was the perceptive, high-scoring England international forward Charlie Buchan, who was appointed team captain. Norris recoiled at Sunderland's transfer fee of £4,000 but agreed to £2,000 up front and £100 for every goal Buchan scored that season. Buchan put away 20 goals, so both sides were content.

Arsenal made a reasonable, if shaky, beginning to Chapman's first season – 1925/26 – until their humiliating 7-0 away defeat by Newcastle. Buchan, in particular, was furious and implored Chapman to adopt a 'stopper' system – moving the centre-half from midfield into defence – to deal with the increased goal opportunities created by the new offside law.

Arsenal's results improved significantly and, boosted by the manager's other positional changes, such as switching Jimmy Brain to centre-forward and the acquisition of speedy outside-right Joe Hulme, they ended the season with 52 points – their highest-ever till then – and were second-placed behind Huddersfield: all in all, a more than satisfactory season for Chapman and Norris.

The following season, 1926/27, was less satisfactory in the League, finishing 11th, but Chapman's team building continued. In came right-back Tom Parker, big centre-forward Jack Lambert and, to provide the role of 'stopper' in this emerging system, tall, red-haired Herbie 'Copper' Roberts who was as effective in the air as he was solid on the ground.

20

'Wembley, Wembley . . .'

In April 1927 Arsenal reached their first FA Cup Final. Prior to this game, they had progressed beyond the fourth round stage on only four other occasions: an undistinguished record for an ambitious club such as Arsenal.

Their opponents at Wembley Stadium were Cardiff City. Over 90,000 spectators turned up to watch a match in which Arsenal, although clearly the more skilful side, could not score against their Welsh opponents, with the soggy surface affecting passing accuracy and ball control.

With around 16 minutes of a goalless game remaining, Cardiff's centre-forward Hugh Ferguson attempted a shot at goal, one which was saved by Arsenal's stand-in keeper Dan Lewis, himself a Welshman. However, when the keeper attempted to avoid the onrushing forward, the ball slipped from Lewis's grasp and rolled under his arm over the goalline. The Final ended 1-0 in favour of Cardiff City.

This result was, and remains to this day, the only time a non-English club has won the FA Cup. After the game, Lewis hurled his loser's medal onto the turf, but it was collected and handed back to him by his Welsh teammate, a consoling Bob John. The goal was blamed on Lewis's shiny new jersey and a greasy ball, with *The Times* describing the goal under the headline 'A tragic blunder'.

A ritual then evolved, whereby for the following thirty years Arsenal goalies wore an unwashed old jersey for their appearances at Wembley Finals.

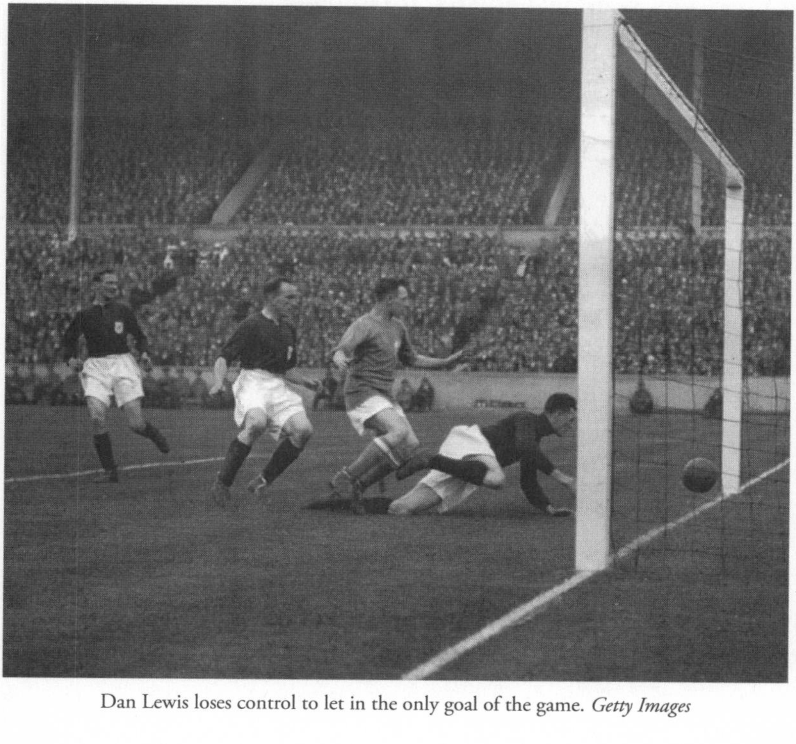

Dan Lewis loses control to let in the only goal of the game. *Getty Images*

21

Something in the air . . .

Earlier in the 1926/27 season, Highbury was the venue for the first ever football match to be broadcast live on radio.

The game was Arsenal v Sheffield United, on Saturday 22 June 1927, just three weeks after the BBC had received a Royal Charter which enabled it to cover major sporting events. *The Radio Times* printed a numbered grid to help listeners follow Henry Wakelam's commentary, and Charlie Buchan scored the first ever broadcast goal in the 1-1 draw.

Three months later, the BBC also aired the first ever live broadcast of the Cup Final, the commentary coming from Arsenal director George Allison.

22

Buchan retires: who'll replace him?

The manager did not appear particularly perturbed by the Cardiff defeat, and still the players arrived at Highbury. Young left-back Eddie Hapgood was settling in, and 29-year-old Tom Whittaker had taken over as head trainer and was becoming a leading and respected physiotherapist. Arsenal again reached the FA Cup semi-final, only to be beaten by Blackburn Rovers, and they ended tenth in the League at the end of 1927/28. The defence was getting used to new players, but they were letting in more goals than the forwards were scoring.

At the end of this season, Charlie Buchan resigned. Chapman's first signing, his captain and his talisman departed Highbury to become a journalist. There was only one conceivable replacement, at least in a goalscoring sense. England international David Jack was a tall, elegant, almost imperious inside-forward, who wore spats and played for Bolton Wanderers. Bolton said he was not available at any price but, soon after this firm refusal, Jack had become an Arsenal player.

Chapman had obtained his man, even though he had to pay a transfer fee of £11,500, which was twice the existing record fee and the first five-figure transfer in UK footballing history. It was around this time that Arsenal were christened 'the Bank of England team', the implication being that the club was attempting to buy success rather than to earn it. Jack's arrival did nothing to dispel this pejorative label, but time was to reveal the intuitive wisdom of Chapman's spending.

Despite Jack's contribution of 25 League goals, in season 1928/29 the club were again knocked out of the FA Cup in the sixth round, and could only manage ninth place in the League. However, Chapman had promised Arsenal a title within five years, 1929/30 was the fifth year, and Chapman was a man of his word.

23

Chapman's team comes together

In May 1929, Chapman acquired from Exeter City an exceptionally gifted 16-year-old inside-left named Cliff Bastin, and moved him to the left wing for his Arsenal debut in October that year. In the coming years 'Boy' Bastin was to make this position his own.

Bastin was followed to Highbury by Alex James, a Scotsman, a 'Wembley Wizard' and an attacking, goalscoring inside-left for Preston North End. The Lancashire team had been described as 'Alex James and ten others'. James was the player Chapman needed at the heart of his new team. He was to become the 'midfield general' of the great Arsenal side of the 1930s.

Both players took time to adjust to their unfamiliar roles in Chapman's new formation, and it was not until the second half of the season that the two newcomers and their teammates began to demonstrate their unity and dominance as a team. In March, Arsenal put four past Manchester United and Blackburn Rovers. In April they beat Sheffield United by an astonishing 8-1, and achieved a scarcely credible 6-6 draw away at Leicester City, a result which remains today as the highest score draw between two top-level teams. Despite these results, they finished 14th in the League, with only a relatively meagre 78 goals scored.

24

Arsenal secure their first trophy

The team's progress in the 1930 FA Cup, however, was very different, and vindicated Chapman's promise of a trophy within five years.

Having fought their way to the FA Cup Final – and been forced into a semi-final replay against Second Division Hull City – Arsenal faced 'the team of the 1920s', Huddersfield Town, with the northern club's hat-trick of First Division League titles (1924-1926) and a 1922 FA Cup victory. Arsenal had won nothing, but had learned much from Huddersfield's ex-mentor Herbert Chapman.

The teams walked out onto the pitch side-by-side (for the first time in a Wembley Final) on 26 April, shook hands with King George V, and the game began. Within 17 minutes James, after a quick passing move with Bastin, opened the scoring. After the massive 'Graf Zeppelin' had drifted overhead and departed, and with ten minutes remaining, Lambert shuffled his way through a couple of defenders and ran the length of Huddersfield's half to score the second. The game ended 2-0 in Arsenal's favour, and they had finally won a major trophy.

Arsenal were the more defensive side during the game, and cries of 'boring Arsenal' were increasingly heard from opposing fans. But although their defence was indeed solid and unyielding, their speed and intelligence on the counter-attack, with Alex James adroitly controlling play from midfield, was often breathtaking, and the pace, movement and striking ability of the forwards – Hulme, Lambert and Bastin – had confused and plundered defences across the country.

James was the man of the match – 'James the master player', as the *Daily Mail* headlined its report – and Arsenal well deserved their victory. Both teams and officials enjoyed dinner together that evening, as if to acknowledge the passing of the baton and to celebrate the arrival of a new era in English football.

The 1930 FA Cup Final team.

Back (left to right): Alf Baker, Jack Lambert, Charlie Preedy, William 'Bill' Seedon, Eddie Hapgood, Robert John.

Middle: Herbert Chapman (Manager), David Jack, Tom Parker (Captain), Alex James, Tom Whittaker (Trainer).

Front: Joe Hulme, Cliff Bastin. *Colorsport*

25

The WM formation

The 2-3-5 formation (two full-backs, three half-backs and five forwards) had been standard in English football since it was adopted successfully by Preston North End in the 1880s. It was, however, manifestly unsuited to the new offside law, and Chapman was one of several managers in the late 1920s who were working on more flexible systems to handle the changed situation.

Chapman was developing a system which was based on the individual capabilities and talents of his players, and their suitability for their roles, as well as on refining the interlinking demands of the format. Initially stimulated by the opinions of Charlie Buchan, who reflected the manager's own long-held views on the game, Chapman had assembled the ideal team for his new formation which, due to its shape on the pitch, became known as 'WM'.

WM involved the following adjustments:

i) the centre-half moving back to defence, and marking the opposing centre-forward while patrolling the centre of defence generally;

ii) the full-backs assuming wider positions and marking wingers rather than inside-forwards;

iii) the inside-forwards dropping back to midfield to control the space which was previously the centre-half's domain, and, crucially, to act as the creative links between defence and attack;

iv) and two fast wingers to create chances for a predatory centre-forward and/or to cut inside full-backs and themselves assume the roles of goalscoring inside-forwards.

This 3-2-2-3 WM formation depended on speedy, intelligent players who understood their roles, and by the early 1930s Chapman had them all in place. In particular, there was no 'playmaker' in British football to match the exceptional, all-round visionary talents of Alex James, the pivot of the team.

It was, at heart, a defensive, counter-attacking layout, but the cool brilliance of James, the devastating pace and finishing of the forwards, and the calm authority of the defence made Arsenal by some distance the team to watch and to emulate as the 1930s progressed.

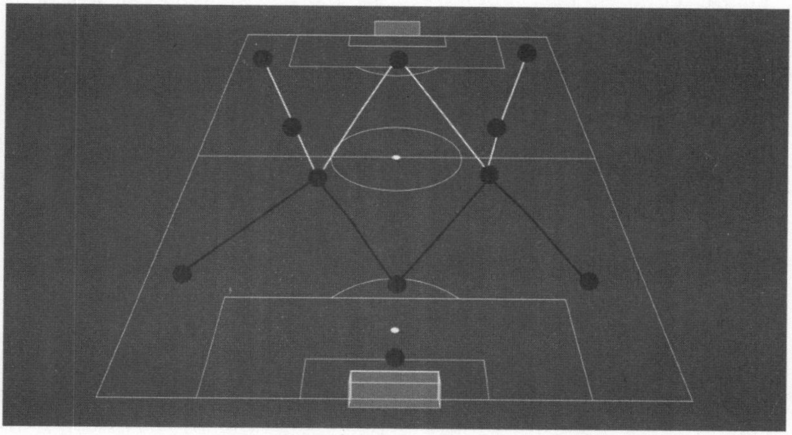

The WM formation. *Mehdi Lahlou, Football-Footprints*

26

The first great season . . .

It all came together in season 1930/31. The Gunners, as Arsenal were becoming known, began their First Division campaign unbeaten in their first nine games. In November they toppled Villa as League leaders. Their victories included a 7-1 defeat of Blackpool in December, a 9-1 thrashing of Grimsby Town in January, a 7-2 hammering of Leicester, and so on it went. Arsenal won seven of their last nine games, and they won the League title at Highbury with two games remaining, finishing 1930/31 seven points ahead of Aston Villa in second place.

The Gunners had claimed the First Division title for the first time in their history, and it was the first League title to have been won by a southern club. They ran up other records: 66 points from a possible 84, were beaten in only four games, failed to score in only one game, and in 17 games they scored four or more goals. Boring Arsenal? Not this year, anyway.

27

. . . and the first great team

The final game of the 1930/31 season – a 5-0 defeat of Bolton Wanderers at Highbury – contained the team which, in the eyes of many, represented Arsenal at their finest in that long-gone era.

In goal was the reliable Ted Harper; the two full-backs were captain Tom Parker and Eddie Hapgood; Herbie Roberts occupied the centre-half role; Charlie Jones and Bob John operated as half-backs; Joe Hulme and Cliff Bastin provided pace and penetration on the wings; Jack Lambert and David Jack were the goalscoring forwards; and the linkman and ball provider was the indispensable Alex James.

There were other equally memorable players acquired over the following couple of years, including the agile England international keeper Frank Moss; George Male, the rugged right-back who partnered Hapgood after Parker's retirement; the two half-backs, Wilf Copping and Jack Crayston, who proved more than adequate replacements for Jones and John; and the prolific centre-forward, Ted Drake. There were others.

Chapman's ability to assess players' skills, his motivational talents, and his awareness of players' appropriate roles on the pitch were fast becoming legendary.

28

'The best laid plans o' mice an' men . . .

. . . Gang aft agley', as Rabbie Burns wrote and as Arsenal's 1931/32 season demonstrated. Chapman had been hoping that this was to be a double year but, in the event, his outstanding team won nothing. A combination of over-confidence, bad luck and injuries was the main problem.

In the League, a bad start proved impossible to overcome and Arsenal ended in second place, two points behind Everton. They did, however, reach the FA Cup Final against Newcastle United, but without the injured Alex James. Just before half-time Arsenal were 1-0 ahead, when a long pass went over their byline. As the defenders turned to trudge back to the centre, a Newcastle winger crossed the ball back into their penalty area, from where Newcastle scored the 'equaliser'. The referee allowed this 'goal' to stand – even though the ball had been entirely out of play – and a disheartened Arsenal let in another in the second half to lose the Final 2-1.

29

Meanwhile, off the pitch . . .

Chapman's innovations – including regular team talks and discussions, and listening closely and acting on his players' comments – were not only confined to his team.

He ordered white sleeves for the all-red shirts and he suggested adding numbers on players' backs, both for purposes of quick, on-pitch identification. The Football League rejected the latter idea, but by the late 1930s numbers were made compulsory.

Perhaps his smartest move was to persuade London Electric Railway (today's London Transport) to change the name of Gillespie Road Underground station to Arsenal station. The station exit sat on the Piccadilly Line across the road from entrances to the North Bank and West Stand. The LER suggested alternative names, such as Highbury Hill, but Chapman was adamant, saying 'this is Arsenal territory'. The station was opened as Arsenal on 5 November 1932, and it remains the only tube station in London to have been named after a football club.

The manager ordered the construction of a 12-foot diameter clock to stand on the North Bank, which was then known as the 'Laundry End' after the old Gillespie Road laundry behind the terracing. The clock was moved in 1935 to sit at the top of the south terrace, which quickly became known as the Clock End. The clock remained there for 70 years until the move to Ashburton Grove.

Chapman also initiated the 1930s redevelopment of the stadium. On previously uncovered terracing appeared the art deco West Stand, with room for over 20,000 spectators, which was opened in 1932. The FA objected to the built-in floodlights which were removed (permanent floodlights were not formally accepted in England until 1950).

The Archibald Leitch stand was demolished, and in its place was erected the East Stand, approached from Avenell Road and which contained the club's main offices, the 'marble halls' and, before it was moved to Ashburton Grove, Jacob Epstein's sculpted bust of Chapman.

The North Bank was roofed over, and the terracing was largely retained. At the foot of the North Bank, in the early 1930s a builder's horse fell into a deeply excavated hole, and it proved impossible to extract the animal. Its body was covered over, but its ghost continues to haunt the North Bank. Or so I'm told.

Up to its closure in 2006, and even after all the changes prompted by the 1990s Taylor Report, Highbury remained, architecturally and socially, one of the friendliest and most welcoming stadiums in England.

30

Back on the pitch

Arsenal began the 1932/33 season with a re-energised Alex James, and new signing Ernie Coleman replacing Lambert. With three games remaining in the League, they played Chelsea away and required a win to reclaim the title. They won 3-1, with two from Bastin, and were again First Division champions. Bastin's tally for the season was 33 League goals, the highest number scored by a winger since the League began.

However, to describe Arsenal's defeat in the third round of the FA Cup that season as 'embarrassing' is seriously to understate what happened. In fact, it was one of the greatest giant-killing performances in the history of British club football. On 14 January 1933 Arsenal travelled to Fellows Park, home to their opponent, Third Division Walsall. Flu had incapacitated Hapgood, Lambert, Coleman and Hulme, so Chapman, confident of an easy win, included four reserve players in the first team. In front of a fiercely partisan West Midland crowd of 11,000, the Saddlers scored twice in the second half for a 2-0 defeat of the mighty Arsenal.

Chapman was outraged at the appalling performance, and he quickly transferred three of the four reserves, blaming them for the debacle. Walsall were eliminated in the next round, but 50 years later they were to repeat their stunning win over Arsenal.

31

Chapman dies

By the 1933/34 season, Chapman realised his squad was ageing, so Ray Bowden replaced Jack, and Ralph Birkett took over from Hulme. In early January 1934, with Arsenal four points clear in the League, 55-year-old Chapman died from a sudden attack of pneumonia. His death was mourned by the world of football and particularly by his players.

Arsenal reacted to the shock of Chapman's death by losing their next three games, but they soon regained their impetus. Not only did they reach the sixth round of the FA Cup, but they also retained the First Division title, ending three points ahead of Huddersfield Town. Arsenal finished that season as, once again, England's dominant football club.

George Allison, whose involvement with the club stretched back to the Woolwich days, was appointed managing director after Chapman's death, but for the rest of that season the daily running of the club was placed in the experienced and capable hands of Tom Whittaker and Joe Shaw.

Although there were numerous applications to take over from Chapman, Allison was offered and accepted the role. And the new manager had not forgotten what Herbert Chapman, shortly before his death, had said to him: 'Mr Allison, we must rebuild.'

Right: The statue to Herbert Chapman at the Emirates stadium. *Alamy*

32

A hard man to follow

Allison began his first full season of 1934/35 with an emphatic 8-1 demolition of Liverpool, with the manager's new signing from Southampton, Ted Drake, netting a hat-trick.

Drake's scoring exploits this season were reinforced by the playmaking James, and by Bastin and Bowden. The recently arrived wing-halves were 'Gentleman Jack' Crayston and Wilf 'Ironman' Copping, their nicknames revealing their respective on-pitch proclivities. The back line remained Male, Roberts and Hapgood, with Moss between the posts.

In January, Arsenal played five games without conceding a goal. The crunch game was at Highbury on 9 March when, with two games in hand over their closest competitor Sunderland, Arsenal drew 0-0 in front of a 73,295 crowd, which remained the old stadium's highest ever attendance for an Arsenal home game. The Gunners lost only one of their ten remaining games, and they clinched their third League title in succession. They did so by scoring 115 goals, 25 more than Sunderland. Ted Drake also set a long-standing record with his 42 League goals.

Allison, Whittaker and the Arsenal players had continued the Herbert Chapman legacy, in a manner which would have delighted that visionary manager.

33

'Too much rough play by visitors'

This was the *Guardian*'s primly understated headline above its report of the England v Italy international 'friendly' played in that historic triple season at Highbury on 14 November 1934. In the eyes of most other observers it was a hostile, violent and brutal confrontation. An England player described the game as 'a battle', which has led to its enduring label as 'The Battle of Highbury'.

It remains the only English international fixture in which seven players from one club – this, of course, being Arsenal – have been selected to start such a match. In this case, these players were Moss, Male, Hapgood, Copping, Bowden, Drake and Bastin. When the final whistle blew, they probably wished they'd been somewhere else.

In the second minute, Drake was involved in a rough tackle which broke Italian centre-half Monti's foot. After 15 minutes Monti had to leave the pitch, and when the Italians realised they were down to ten men (no substitutes then), they went out for revenge, particularly as they were also 3-0 behind.

The subsequent mayhem was mainly caused by the Italians, who had won the World Cup only five months previously, and the punching and kicking was aimed at anyone wearing an England shirt. Although Italy pulled back two goals in the second half, they were beaten 3-2 by a country which seemed to consider the World Cup a minor event, fit only for foreigners. Meanwhile, the

English dressing room resembled a field hospital. Hapgood had a broken nose, Bowden a badly damaged ankle, Drake's leg was 'cut to ribbons', and this was only for starters.

The press decided that the match had been the 'real' World Cup Final, and expressed doubts about the wisdom of playing any further 'foreign' teams. Italy won the World Cup again in 1938. When England deigned to enter the tournament in 1950, they were defeated by Spain and the USA, and eliminated in the first round.

34

Another FA Cup in the boardroom

As season 1935/36 began, Arsenal were still regarded as a formidable club but, although they remained more than capable of outstanding performances, a sense of anti-climax was also becoming apparent at Highbury.

Other teams – such as Everton, Manchester City, and Wolves – had learnt from Arsenal's successes, and these teams were now serious rivals and title contenders. Some crucial members of Chapman's original squad, such as James and Roberts, were now veterans and were losing the speed and perception of their earlier years, and the injury list was an increasing problem.

Although attendances at Highbury remained impressive, and George Allison was an effective, hard-working manager, he lacked Chapman's intuitive footballing instinct and player empathy. Also, his ability to discover suitable replacements for his ageing squad was less acute than that of Chapman.

In April 1936, however, Arsenal won their second FA Cup, defeating Second Division Sheffield United 1-0 at Wembley. As George Allison said in *The Arsenal Stadium Mystery*: 'It's 1-0 to the Arsenal. That's the way we like it.' Drake scored the winning goal, but Sheffield had the better of the play and deserved to win. In the League, Arsenal finished in sixth place, their lowest position for several years. Drake was again leading goalscorer, and earlier that season he had produced an extraordinary performance.

35

Drake hits a perfect seven

On 14 December 1935 at Villa Park, Arsenal faced an Aston Villa team containing six internationals. The Gunners had been undefeated in their previous six League encounters, but were missing James and Hulme and, although their lead scorer Drake was injured and sporting a knee strap, he played the game of his life.

By half-time, Drake had three shots at goal and had scored with all three. After 60 minutes he had three further shots, and had secured a double hat-trick. Arsenal were now 6-0 ahead and Drake was being marked by virtually the entire Villa defence. However, that day he was exhibiting the ball control and unerringly accurate shooting power of the perfect centre-forward, and there was little the Villa players could do to contain him.

His seventh shot hit the crossbar and his eighth attempt was saved. In the final minute, he latched on to another long ball from Bastin, and he scored again. During his masterclass, Drake scored seven goals from nine shots. Arsenal, or rather Drake, had beaten their old foe Aston Villa 7-1. To this day, Drake's feat has never been equalled at the top level of English football. It's interesting to speculate what he could have done without an injured leg.

36

Gunners again capture title

Two wins from their first nine games was an inauspicious start to 1936/37, but by mid-season Arsenal were again hovering around the top of the League. A late run by Manchester City, picking up 36 points from a possible 40, however, condemned Arsenal to third place at the end of the season. That was also the season which saw the retirement of Herbie Roberts and John, and even the once immortal Alex James succumbed to his weary limbs.

However, as soon as one writes off Arsenal's chances, it's a sound bet that what happens next will prove the error of one's predictions, and that's what happened in 1937/38. The season did not begin particularly well but they again went on a run, and by Easter they topped the League on goal average from this season's bad guys, Wolves. On the last day of the season, Arsenal beat Preston 4-0 at Highbury, while Sunderland defeated Wolves 1-0.

This day of high drama meant that Arsenal had won the League by one point, their fifth and last League title of the 1930s. Although their points achieved (52) was the lowest winning tally in the First Division for almost 20 years, they had still achieved more than any other club that season. It was certainly more than they picked up in the final pre-war season of 1938/39, when they ended the campaign in fifth spot and were knocked out in the third round of the FA Cup.

One player does not make a team. However, Allison's

desperate attempts but ultimate failure to find a 'new' Alex James was a major contributory factor to the Gunners' relative decline in the late 1930s. And without the presence of Herbert Chapman, it's more than probable that none of this would have happened anyway.

The 1937/38 team.

Back (left to right): Sidney Cartwright, William Crayston, Herbert Roberts, Frank Boulton, George Male, Ted Drake, Tom Whittaker (trainer).

Front row: Alfred Kirchen, George Hunt, Eddie Hapgood, George Allison (manager) Leslie Jones, Cliff Bastin, Wilfred Copping. *Colorsport*

37

The Arsenal Stadium Mystery

Highbury Stadium and Arsenal were selected as the backdrop for a 1939 feature film, *The Arsenal Stadium Mystery*. It was based on the book of the same title by the prolific crime novelist L R Gribble, whose only other venture into football was his 1950 book *They Kidnapped Stanley Matthews*.

The plot hinges on the death, in front of 70,000 Highbury spectators, of a player from a fictional top amateur side, the Trojans, in a game against the 1939 Arsenal side, and the investigation by Inspector Slade into the murder. The film was directed by Thorold Dickinson at Highbury Stadium, with the on-pitch scenes mainly shot at Brentford FC's ground. Cliff Bastin, Eddie Hapgood and other team members played themselves, and manager George Allison had a small speaking role.

The film has been subsequently praised by critics as diverse as Martin Scorsese ('exhilarating') and Graham Greene, who praised the director's 'wit of cunning'. Highbury was then one of the few, if not the only, football stadium in Britain to have laid claim to such cinematic distinction.

38

World War Two at White Hart Lane

Shortly after war was declared against Germany on 3 September 1939, Highbury was declared an Air Raid Protection post. A large barrage balloon was erected at the Clock End, and the North Bank was badly damaged by bombing. All Arsenal home games were played at the Tottenham ground, which is four miles to the north.

Most of the squad was called up, and the Football League was halted, but regional competitions sprang up and, meaningless though they were, they flourished. As the war continued, older players – including Alf Kirchen, Jack Crayston, Eddie Hapgood and Ted Drake – retired from playing.

They were gradually making way for left-winger Denis Compton, centre-forward Reg Lewis, versatile full-back Walley Barnes, Scottish inside-forward Jimmy Logie and others. Of the pre-war team, there remained only Cliff Bastin, and defenders George Male and Bernard Joy. (Joy, incidentally, was the last amateur footballer to have played for the English international team.)

Then, at the end of the first post-war season, Bastin, one of Arsenal's and England's all-time greats, also decided to hang up his boots. One of the most skilful wingers and deadliest finishers in the game's history, he had terrorised defences across England in his 392 Arsenal appearances, and his 178 goals remained a club record until broken by Ian Wright and then by Thierry Henry.

39

'Passovotchka' at Highbury

Back at Highbury, in November 1945 an Arsenal team – including Bastin and Joy, as well as such 'guests' as Stan Matthews and Stan Mortensen – played Dynamo Moscow on the Soviet club's brief UK tour.

A large crowd of 55,000 attended the game as, with organised European club football a decade away, these were mysterious visitors. Dense fog reduced visibility to 20 yards, which didn't help the spectators but allowed Dynamo briefly to field 12 men. The game was acrimonious and disagreement was frequent, not helped by the ref and linesmen being, at Dynamo's insistence, appointed by them.

However, no one could argue about the high quality of the Soviet club's fast interlinking and one-touch passing game, described as 'passovotchka'. Despite the worsening weather conditions, Dynamo insisted on playing to the end, and they won 4-3, although there was some dispute over the identities of the scorers.

The game's general air of distrust and suspicion, on both sides, was supposedly what prompted George Orwell to describe sport as 'war minus the fighting'.

40

Tom Whittaker takes over

George Allison, Arsenal's increasingly jaded manager, took advantage of a dispute between the player and his club Everton to lure the 33-year-old England international defender Joe Mercer to Highbury, along with 35-year-old centre-forward Ronnie Rooke from Fulham. In spite of the new talent, Arsenal ended up in 13th position at the season's finish, and Allison resigned as manager.

Tom Whittaker had long been a much respected and popular figure at Highbury. He was appointed the new manager, and he quickly repayed the trust which the club had demonstrated in his managerial potential.

He bought right-winger Don Roper and right-half Archie Macauley, and Arsenal won their first six games of 1947/48. As Whittaker's first season progressed, so too did Arsenal's title challenge. Under the captaincy of Joe Mercer, with George Swindin in goal, the return of Jimmy Logie, Les Compton as centre-half and his brother Denis on the left wing, and the high-scoring Rooke and Lewis up front, Arsenal again won the League title, this time by seven points.

The following couple of League seasons were, by Arsenal's previous standards, not particularly noteworthy, with finishes in fifth and sixth place. Although Whittaker brought in another three forwards – Doug Lishman, Freddie Cox and Peter Goring, the last to replace Crystal Palace-bound Ronnie Rooke – the team displayed little of their old consistency, but they perked up in the FA Cup in 1949/50. In fact, they again reached Wembley, where the opposition was Liverpool.

Two goals from Lewis made sure of a 2-0 victory and Arsenal's third FA Cup trophy and, as *The Times* commented: 'Seldom can Arsenal have performed as well this season.'

The 1949/50 FA Cup-winning team.

Back (left to right): Tom Whittaker (manager), Laurie Scott, George Swindin, Walley Barnes, William Milne (trainer).

Front row: Denis Compton, Peter Goring, Alex Forbes, Joe Mercer, Reg Lewis, Leslie Compton.

Ground: Jimmy Logie, Freddie Cox. *Colorsport*

41

'To Arsenal, the glory'

With keeper Swindin and big Doug Lishman injured for most of the following season, the Gunners finished in fifth spot, 13 points behind first-time winners Spurs. In 1951/52, Arsenal were leading the League by Christmas but a growing injury list and fixture congestion did not aid their cause. At the season's end they were in third place behind Spurs and Manchester United.

One week later, the tired players arrived at Wembley for the FA Cup Final against Newcastle, but an injury to Walley Barnes meant they were forced to play with ten men for most of the game. They displayed a heroic defence and almost scored on the counterattack, but with only seven fit Arsenal players on the pitch, Newcastle netted with five minutes left for a 1-0 victory. Arsenal were widely praised and the Newcastle vice-chairman commented: 'To us the Cup; to Arsenal the glory.'

42

Floodlights at Highbury

At the start of the previous season, Arsenal played their first floodlit game at Highbury, bringing to fruition Chapman's vision of almost two decades previously. Israeli club Hapoel Tel Aviv were the first to experience this atmosphere, and a crowd of 50,000 turned up to watch Hapoel's 6-1 defeat.

There were several other such floodlit friendlies at Highbury and these were popular events, the next game seeing 10,000 turned away from a fixture against Rangers.

Daytime matches, too, were pulling in the crowds, particularly in 1952/53. Knocked out of the FA Cup in the sixth round by Blackpool, by mid-April Arsenal were heading the League, but it developed into a close three-way race involving Preston and Wolves.

On the evening before the FA Cup Final – 1 May, 1953 – Arsenal lined up against Burnley at Highbury, knowing that they had to win in order to capture the First Division title for the seventh time in their history. A draw would see the title going to Preston.

Watched by a 51,000 crowd, within four minutes Joe Mercer's own goal was cancelled by a Forbes strike. By half-time, Logie and Lishman added two more. With 15 minutes remaining, Burnley pulled one back but Swindin and Mercer were solid in defence, with Mercer noting 'we played 4-2-4 with a vengeance'.

The final whistle blew, and Arsenal had beaten Burnley 3-2. They had also won the League by 0.099 of a goal, the smallest winning margin in First Division history.

The 1952/53 First Division champions.

Back (left to right): Jack Crayston, Arthur Shaw, Don Oakes, Cliff Holton, Arthur Milton, Jack Kelsey, Bill Dodgin, Peter Goring, Len Wills, Reuben Marden, J Shaw, W Milne

Front (left to right): Joe Wade, Don Roper, Lionel Smith, Alex Forbes, Tom Whittaker (manager), Jimmy Logie, Doug Lishman, Wally Barnes, Dave Bowen. *Alamy*

43

A long wait until the next one

After the Burnley game, the Arsenal support joyfully celebrated the title win, but their enthusiasm may have been less exuberant had they known that it was going to take Arsenal 17 years to claim their next trophy.

Arsenal lost six of the first eight League matches in 1953/54, including a comprehensive 7-1 away hammering by Sunderland. After the Sunderland game, Jack Kelsey – a keeper reputed to possess the biggest hands in English football – replaced Swindin, but not even Kelsey's massive mitts could prevent the team ending in 12th position.

In April, Mercer broke his leg in an on-pitch collision at Highbury. As he was being carried off on a stretcher, he rose and waved to the crowd. The 40-year-old team captain, who had made 247 Arsenal appearances, knew his time was up. He received a heartfelt standing ovation.

The arrival of famed (but ageing) English international centre-forward Tommy Lawton in September 1955 did little to halt the team's decline. Jimmy Logie and Doug Lishman left the club, but younger players, such as forwards Vic Groves, David Herd and Jimmy Bloomfield were taking their places. Arsenal's fifth spot at the end of 1955/56, having won seven of their final eight games, was achieved by younger, if less mature, players.

If the youthful rejuvenation of Arsenal was Tom Whittaker's

idea, he was unable to see it through, as he died from a heart attack in October 1956. Denis Compton, a friend and player, said of Whittaker: 'He was a great and kindly man.' This sentiment was echoed by those who knew and worked with him.

Joe Mercer is carried from the field after breaking his leg against Liverpool at Highbury. *Alamy*

44

What is to be done?

The ten years following the death of Whittaker saw the hiring and firing of three managers, none of whom brought much in the way of success or trophies to Highbury.

Arsenal's declining situation was exacerbated by the emergence of Tottenham who, throughout the 1960s, eclipsed Arsenal. Spurs were the first Double side of the 20th century and were London's leading team during that decade. Although the Gunners fielded some undeniably talented players, there was a general lack of purpose and team understanding at Highbury over these years.

In the immediate aftermath of Whittaker's death, ex-player Jack Crayston assumed the managerial role. In his only full season in charge, Crayston's team ended 12th in the League, having also been humiliated and beaten by Third Division Northampton Town in the third round of the FA Cup. However, the following month Arsenal came close to defeating Manchester United, First Division winners in the previous two seasons.

45

'Busby Babes' entertain Highbury

On 1 February 1958, Matt Busby's much praised, thrilling young Manchester United side met Arsenal at Highbury in the League. By all accounts, both sides contributed to one of the most exciting exhibitions of attacking play to have been seen in English football for a long while.

By half-time, United were 3-0 ahead but, within twelve minutes of the restart, Arsenal levelled through a Herd volley and two from Broomfield. United upped the score to 5-3, Arsenal made it 5-4, and that was the final result.

In hindsight, it was, to say the least, a poignant clash, as it was the last game this particular Manchester United side played in England before the Munich air crash, in which eight of the team died.

46

Swindin becomes manager

A disillusioned Crayston resigned as manager in May 1958, his role taken by another Arsenal ex-player, George Swindin. The one-time Arsenal keeper got rid of a few players, and he brought in from Preston the abrasive half-back Tommy Docherty. In his first season, 1958/59, the team were placed third in the League – a definite improvement – but 1959/60 was again disappointing. Not helped by a series of injuries to key players, Arsenal ended the season in 11th place. Their demoralisation was compounded by neighbours Spurs' triumph in the League.

Inside-left George Eastham had fallen out with his club Newcastle over its insistence on the archaic 'retain and transfer' system – finally repealed in 1963 – and he arrived at Highbury midway through the 1960/61 season. Another newcomer was 19-year-old half-back, Terry Neill. On Eastham's arrival Bloomfield left the club, as did Tommy Docherty for a coaching job at Chelsea. But Arsenal remained in mid-table, as they did in 1961/62.

Swindin, a manager prone to constant but largely ineffective changes of players, was the next manager to depart. In his place, in May 1962, there was appointed a true English football superstar.

47

And now . . . Billy Wright

When someone like Billy knocks at your door, you let him in before he changes his mind. He had enjoyed a remarkable football career: captaining Wolves three times to the League title, gaining a record 105 English international caps with 90 of them as captain, and being voted Footballer of the Year. He was also a CBE, and he was married to one of the country's biggest pop stars, Joy Beverley. May I take your coat, Mr Wright?

However, he had no previous football managerial experience, which was something of a drawback. But he did possess at Highbury some more than capable players, including Strong and Eastham up front, flanked on the wings by Skirton and the teenage George Armstrong. He also understood the supporters' and club's need, in these hard times, for a charismatic, goalscoring centre-forward, so he moved quickly on this front.

The first English player to be capped for his country while playing outside the English League – in his case, Hibs – Joe Baker was Wright's first signing. The transfer fee paid to the 22-year-old's team Torino was an Arsenal record £70,000 (and Torino were happy to unload Baker, fed up as they were with his Italian antics with his pal Denis Law). Baker displayed his skills to good effect in his partnership at Highbury with Geoff Strong in 1962/63, scoring 52 goals between them, although defensive shortcomings saw Arsenal end seventh that season.

48

The Fairs Cup

The Inter-Cities Fairs Cup began in 1955. Known as the Fairs Cup, it was the first pan-European club competition, as previous tournaments, such as the Mitropa Cup, had concentrated on specific geographical areas within the continent.

Lacking the grandeur of its contemporary, the European Cup, it was nonetheless a significantly easier route into Europe for less successful clubs. In 1971 it ceased trading, making way for the UEFA Cup, today's Europa League. Arsenal's seventh placing in 1962/63 was sufficiently elevated to qualify, for the first time, for European competition in 1963/64. Although they were eliminated in the second round of the tournament by RFC Liege, they had developed a taste for the competition, and this would be emphatically confirmed in six years' time.

49

It gets worse . . .

It has been wisely observed that supporters are proud of their team when it is succeeding, but they fall in love with their team when it is suffering. This is true, but only up to a point. The end of the Wright era was drawing closer but the patience of the fans was being increasingly tested. The manager, however, was slowly assembling a winning side, although it may not have appeared so on the pitch.

In that season of 1963/64 Baker and Strong were again rampant in front of goal, claiming 31 apiece, but the defence still leaked goals. Big centre-half Ian Ure was acquired from Dundee but Arsenal could contrive only eighth position in the League.

The following year witnessed the arrival of two men – right-back Don Howe and attacking wing-half Frank McLintock – who were to be instrumental in reviving the fortunes of this sleeping giant of a club. Younger players at the club, including John Radford, Peter Simpson and Jon Sammels, were also about to play their parts in the club's reawakening. Arsenal ended the season 13th in the League and were knocked out of the FA Cup by lowly Peterborough United.

Season 1965/66 was even worse. Although Arsenal were joined by staunch defender Peter Storey (another long-term linchpin), Joe Baker – top scorer for four successive years – upped and went to Nottingham Forest. Arsenal concluded this disastrous term with 12 wins from a possible 42, 14th place in the League and were eliminated by Blackburn Rovers in the third round of the FA Cup.

Wright had lost control of the dressing room. He had been too easy-going and genial with players, some of whom were increasingly disputatious. The supporters had also endured enough. This latter disaffection was obvious at Highbury in the penultimate game of the season, on 5 May 1966, when the stadium's lowest-ever attendance – 4,544 spectators – turned up for a match against Leeds, who won 3-0.

Billy Wright 'resigned' to become Head of Sport at ABC TV. His replacement as manager could not have been more different.

50

'Use the 'ammer, 'Enry'

Three weeks later, ten times as many fans filled Highbury Stadium. But, alas, they had not turned up to watch the toiling Gunners. On the evening of 21 May 1966, British boxer Henry Cooper was the attraction. Henry's opponent? World Heavyweight Champion, Muhammed Ali, until recently Cassius Clay.

Cooper was an Arsenal fan and trained with the club's players and physios, so the Gunner fans turned up to support him, although few in the crowd reckoned he had much of a chance against the 'Louisville Lip', the man who was to become the 20th century's finest and most controversial boxer.

Sure enough, Henry lasted six rounds, but a bad cut above his eye forced the ref to stop the fight and to declare Ali the winner. Ali was a boxer who was simply several leagues above Henry, but Henry gave it all he had and he remained a Gunners hero.

51

Moving on up

Few people were as surprised as Bertie Mee when, in June 1966, he was asked to take over as Arsenal's new manager. Mee had been the club's physio for the previous six years, but he'd never been a manager. A determined fellow, though, he persuaded his friend Dave Sexton, a footballing man to his bootlaces, to work directly with the players while Mee looked after everything else.

Sexton's vision of a sound and solid defence, a creative midfield and a fast, attacking forward line made sense to Mee, so they began season 1966/67 in tandem. Mee preferred hard workers to individualistic creative players, so Eastham and Skirton were speedily transferred. The attention was switched to the younger players already at the club, including Armstrong, Radford, Sammels and Simpson. As the season progressed, voluble full-back Bob McNab and languid, goalscoring George 'Stroller' Graham joined the arrivals.

The team began well that first season but then slumped alarmingly, although an unbeaten final 12 games gave Arsenal a fairly respectable seventh place. In the second season, Sexton decamped to manage Chelsea. In came 'no nonsense', ex-Arsenal defender Don Howe to replace him and to stamp his authority on the players. Young full-back Pat Rice and Bob Wilson, a teacher in next-door Holloway School and a fine goalkeeper, were also coming through the ranks. Alongside the more experienced Storey and McLintock, the 'Double' team was taking shape, although ninth in the League that season did not indicate much in the way of progress.

Mee's team's performance in the League Cup that season was more promising. Arsenal reached the Final at Wembley in March, only to lose 1-0 in an unpleasant game to Don Revie's dominant but deeply cynical Leeds United. In Mee's third season, the Gunners kicked off their League campaign with a 2-1 defeat of Spurs at White Hart Lane. Suitably encouraged, they embarked on a nine-game unbeaten run and then faded, but they improved their final League position to fourth which gave them entry to the 1969/70 Fairs Cup.

Bertie Mee. *Alamy*

52

Savaged by Swindon

The League Cup Final, at Wembley on 15 March 1969, is still remembered as one of the several deeply embarrassing results in Arsenal's history.

Arsenal's defeat in the previous season's League Cup Final was at least at the hands of one of England's top sides, Leeds United, so no shame there. This year's Final was against Third Division Swindon Town, surely a walkover for Arsenal. In the event, a first-half, badly mistimed back-pass from Ian Ure to Bob Wilson gave Swindon a 1-0 lead, and it was only a last-minute error by Swindon's otherwise excellent keeper which prevented a dramatic Swindon 90-minute victory. Even worse, in extra-time two goals from Swindon's Don Rogers – running half the length of the pitch for the third – led to a 3-1 victory for Swindon and to abject humiliation for Arsenal.

Although most of the Arsenal players were suffering the after-effects of flu, and the wet conditions at Wembley had sapped their energy, this was an enormous upset and the players were devastated at their performance and at such headlines as 'Arsenal's Shame'.

53

At last, an Arsenal trophy

Changes, therefore, were necessary for 1969/70, and the frequently hapless Ian Ure was transferred to Manchester United. It had been one defensive mistake too many for Ure.

Young, local centre-forward Charlie George made his first-team debut in the season's opener, but Arsenal managed only one win from their first 12 games and were knocked out in the third round of the FA Cup. Another forward, Ray Kennedy, made his first appearance in January and, with young players such as the quick, elusive Eddie Kelly in midfield, Arsenal managed 12th in the League.

This season was again, however, about the Fairs Cup. After these 17 barren years, Arsenal had to win something and even a virtually redundant European trophy would suffice. They stumbled through the opening rounds but kept going. In this home and away tournament, their victims – a parade of the celebrated and the mundane – included Glentoran, Sporting Lisbon, Rouen, Dinamo Bacau, the soon-to-be unbeatable Ajax, and they met Anderlecht in game one of the Final in late April 1970 in Belgium. Anderlecht were a fast, attacking side starring Jan Mulders and Paul Van Himst. The Belgians were 3-0 ahead until Kennedy scored with his first touch, and the game ended 3-1 to Anderlecht.

It was a different Arsenal performance a week later in the second leg at Highbury, as if the players were determined to set the trophy hoodoo to rest. A re-energised team opened the scoring with a first-half Eddie Kelly strike and, midway through the second half, the increasingly confident Radford made it 2-0 with a header. Within two minutes Sammels made the score 3-0. Arsenal held on, and at the game's end they had won 3-0 and picked up their first trophy in 17 years. Joy was, as they say, unconfined, and Arsenal had deserved to win a major victory. At long last.

The Times described the evening as '. . . a night every Arsenal supporter will remember . . . they have waited long enough.'

Ajax's Johan Cruyff battles for the ball with Frank McLintock during the Fairs Cup semi-final first leg at Highbury. *Colorsport*

54

The Double season: preamble

Before the 1970/71 campaign began, the bookies' money was on the team of the moment – Don Revie's Leeds United – to win the League, with Chelsea and Everton close behind. As for Arsenal, they may have won last season's Fairs Cup (doesn't everyone?) but they were 12th in the League and had been knocked out of the FA Cup in the third round. Arsenal? Give me a break.

But at Highbury the mood was much more confident. Never mind the English First Division or the FA Cup. Arsenal had just beaten, over two legs, two of the best and most admired sides in European football. The self-belief of this fast-improving Arsenal team – a combination of assured talented youth, such as George and Radford, and the more experienced players like Graham, Storey and Wilson – was at its peak.

Captain Frank McLintock stated that 'this is the best Arsenal side in my six years at the club' and, though some of them had off-days during the forthcoming season, it was hard to see a weak link in the team. The board and players were understandably tiring of the comparisons with the 1930s side, and winning the League would ditch these fading memories. Some more adventurous souls were even contemplating the Double of League and FA Cup. After all, Spurs – curse them – had shown ten years previously that it was possible. Why couldn't Arsenal do it?

The players were itching for the start of season 1970/71, partly to demolish the critics' dismissive opinions but mainly to show that Arsenal was firmly back where it belonged: at the very top of English football.

55

Season 1970/71: one to remember

Arsenal's first couple of games were away draws at Everton and West Ham, as if the players, given the expectations, were edgy. Storey was moved to midfield to cover Alan Ball, and Rice switched to full-back, positions they occupied for the remainder of the season. The performances were marred by Charlie George suffering a broken ankle in the Everton match and facing a six-month absence from the game.

They won the next two games, but narrowly lost to Chelsea and then were encouraged by holding 'mighty' Leeds to an ugly 0-0 draw at Highbury, with McNab sent off after deliberate provocations by Revie's shock troops. Mee defended his players' behaviour, saying: 'This was the best performance I have ever seen by an Arsenal team against a side the calibre of Leeds.'

After the Leeds game, Arsenal, emboldened by the result, embarked on an unbeaten (except for one) run which lasted for 17 games, including only three draws, and was halted only by Huddersfield away in mid-January 1971, which was followed by a 2-0 Liverpool away defeat two weeks later.

Although in this run they had defeated such sides as Spurs, Everton, Derby, Wolves and West Ham, Arsenal had been decisively spanked 0-5 away by Stoke City in late September.

Stoke were a tough side, emphasised by their 2-0 lead over Arsenal at half-time. For whatever reason, Wilson was uncharacteristically nervous and was responsible, along with his defence, for the final scoreline. It was a strange result for a side who were to be unbeaten in their next 14 matches, but these things happen in football.

56

A punch-up with Lazio

UEFA had decided that, beginning from this season, the winners of the previous year's Fairs Cup would be admitted into the following year's tournament. Arsenal were back in Europe, at a time when, in terms of their domestic ties, they could have done without more games in their crowded schedule. But maybe the Treble?

On 18 September Arsenal, surrounded by flares, fireworks and an intimidating atmosphere, walked uncertainly into Rome's Olympic Stadium to face Lazio – whose most prominent supporter had been Italy's Fascist wartime leader, Benito Mussolini – in their first round, first leg of the Fairs Cup. The club had never before faced an Italian team in competition.

Although Arsenal were 2-0 ahead early in the second half and, to their surprise were the dominant side, the Italians' star striker Giorgio Chinaglia scored twice in the last six minutes for a final 2-2 result. It had been a good game, and the players on both sides seemed friendly enough.

However, it all kicked off at the two clubs' post-match dinner in a ristorante in the heart of Rome. During the meal Ray Kennedy went outside for some air, and he was unaccountably attacked by a Lazio player. Mayhem then erupted. The Lazio players started picking fights inside the restaurant, and then outside. Armstrong was hurled against the team bus, Peter

Marinello was chucked over a car, McNab was pinned against an iron grille, and so it continued. They even tried it on with McLintock, not a wise thing to do.

Mee, a small but determined man, used a combination of persuasion and force to scramble his players, now as wired-up as the Italians, into the team coach, and sped away into the Roman night. Either Kennedy had made an ill-chosen remark to the Lazio player (unlikely) or the Italians were making a point about Arsenal's superiority on the pitch (more likely). Whatever the reason, UEFA fined Lazio for their players' behaviour that evening.

57

Exit from Fairs Cup

A large crowd of 53,000 turned up at Highbury the following week for the return Lazio game. Most were there to watch a famed team of top Italian footballers, but no doubt more than a few came along for a return punch-up. They were both, however, disappointed, as the Italians slunk away after a 2-0 defeat by the Gunners. Storey, a reliable if temper-prone midfielder, created both goals, one for Radford and the other for crowd favourite Geordie Armstrong, resulting in a 4-2 aggregate win for Arsenal. (As an aside, Lazio were relegated from Serie A at the season's end. It obviously doesn't pay to start a bit of bother with the Gunners.)

The next two rounds resulted in 2-1 and 4-0 victories for the Gunners. The second-round, second-leg tie against Austria's Sturm Graz was at Highbury on 4 November and was a cliff-hanger. Storey – again, and enjoying a highly effective season – had to hold his nerve when taking an injury-time penalty. If he scored, Arsenal were through. He scored.

They then disposed of Belgian part-timers Beveren 6-0 on aggregate, and in the quarter-final Arsenal lined up against West German's Koln. They won the first leg 2-1, Storey again scoring the winner. In the second leg in Koln on 23 March, a brutally disgraceful display by the West Germans saw Rice, George and Kennedy receiving bookings, and Arsenal losing 1-0. Bertie Mee was furious at Koln's deliberately provocative behaviour which resulted in his players' bookings, and he slammed the 'childish histrionics' of the West Germans. But Arsenal were now out of the Fairs Cup on the basis of one away goal.

Frank McLintock, right, shakes hands with Koln captain Wolfgang Overath at Highbury. *Colorsport*

58

But there's still the FA Cup . . .

As Arsenal had been eliminated from the League Cup by Crystal Palace in November, there was now only the League and the FA Cup left as the season progressed.

However, this meant a reduction in the number of remaining matches and, with fewer draining games to play, the prospect of achieving the Double came back into focus. Winning the League and the FA Cup in the same season would certainly lay to rest the ghost of the 1930s team. With Arsenal's reinvigorated players, and barring any major injuries to their small but tenacious squad, they could do it.

Arsenal's first game in the third round of the 1970/71 FA Cup was in January against reputed 'giant-killers' Yeovil Town, but the game turned out to be a 3-0 stroll for the Gunners. The fourth round tie was against Portsmouth and 40,000 of their fans at Fratton Park, and it was an altogether tougher assignment. Arsenal squeezed a 1-1 draw and a replay at Highbury on 1 February. Charlie George had returned from injury, replaced an off-form Graham and scored a beauty. In a dirty, messy game, the hero was again Storey, who scored the winner from the penalty spot in the 3-2 win.

A couple more from Charlie George finished off Manchester City in the fifth round, and they met Leicester City in the quarter-final. Arsenal were lucky to leave Filbert Street with a 0-0 draw but in the Highbury replay, a George header was the difference between the teams, and Arsenal had reached the semi-final.

Charlie George (#11) celebrates scoring his first goal past grounded City goalkeeper Joe Corrigan at Maine Road. *Colorsport*

59

Not Stoke again . . .

The 1971 FA Cup semi-final, played on the neutral ground of Hillsborough on 27 March, pitched Arsenal against the one team who had hammered them that season in the League – Stoke City.

Although Stoke ended the season in 13th place, they seemed to reserve their best performances – and there weren't that many of these – for the boys from London N5. Due mainly to defensive jitters, Arsenal were 2-0 down at half-time.

Step forward, once more, our hero Peter Storey, who scored in the 60th minute. And, yet again, in injury time he was faced with a penalty which he had to convert. With Bob Wilson on his knees in prayer in the Arsenal goalmouth, Storey sent Stoke and England keeper Gordon Banks the wrong way for a 2-2 draw. Wilson nearly fainted from relief, and off they all trooped for the replay at Villa Park four days later.

At the Villa Park game, Stoke were but a pale shadow of their previous role as Arsenal's near-nemesis. The Potters rolled over to a superior Arsenal side, and Graham and Kennedy ensured a 2-0 win for the Gunners and a place in the FA Cup Final against Liverpool. After the match, a delighted Mee said to his team: 'You have the chance to put your names in the record books for all time.' The exhausted but elated players realised that Mee was proposing the Double, and they resolved that this would also be the greatest season in the long history of Arsenal Football Club.

60

The League title: Leeds or Arsenal?

After consecutive League defeats in January by Huddersfield and Liverpool, Arsenal won their next two games, were beaten 2-0 away by Derby County at the end of February, and won the following nine games, until West Brom managed a draw. This winning run included an early-April game at Highbury in front of a more-than-capacity crowd of over 62,000 and which Arsenal won 2-0, both goals coming from top scorer Kennedy.

The third-last game of that League season, on 26 April, was crucial, as it was at Elland Road against close title rivals Leeds United. The 48,000 crowd watched a tight and frequently unpleasant contest. Leeds won 1-0, and Mee commented 'never was a defeat less deserved'. There were many who agreed with him. The Gunners then played and won their penultimate match. Arsenal now had a game in hand over Leeds, who had completed their fixture list.

If Arsenal won their last match, the League title would be theirs. This being a book about Arsenal, there are no prizes available for guessing the identity of the club the Gunners had to play in their final League game, the club's most important game for nearly 20 years. It was, of course, their main rival and enemy, Tottenham Hotspur.

61

Mullery awarded Crown Jewels

If any drivers thought they'd take a short cut home along Tottenham High Road on the evening of Monday 3 May 1970, they'd made a serious mistake. Tens of thousands of would-be spectators thronged the streets around White Hart Lane. Even the ref had to dump his car and walk the last mile to the Spurs stadium.

A capacity crowd of almost 52,000 packed into the ground to watch what *The Times* described as 'a magnificent battle in which attack from both sides was the order of the day'. It was a pulsating match, in which little love was lost and no quarter was expected nor given. Spurs' Alan Mullery had summed up his team's attitude when before the game he commented, 'Arsenal have got as much chance of being handed the title by Spurs as I have of being given the Crown Jewels'.

This absorbing contest remained goalless, mainly due to the heroics of Bob Wilson and his defenders until, with three minutes left, Pat Jennings knocked away a Radford cross, but only as far as winger Armstrong. Geordie sent in another cross which Kennedy headed firmly into the net. Spurs made determined attempts to equalise, but the final whistle soon went and Arsenal had won the League. I leave it to you to imagine the unbridled celebrations.

62

And now for the Scousers . . .

Five days later, in front of a crowd of 100,000 on a hot day at Wembley, Arsenal took on Liverpool in the 1971 FA Cup Final. Liverpool were not yet the leading English club in European football, but they were nonetheless a side with such quality players as Steve Heighway, John Toshack and Ray Clemence.

Both sides were constantly on the attack but the game inexorably moved into extra time. Heighway, taking advantage of an uncharacteristic Arsenal defensive muddle, put Liverpool 1-0 ahead. Just before the end of extra time's first period, Kelly equalised, shooting through the legs of the tiring Liverpool defence. With nine minutes remaining, and a replay looming, Charlie George unleashed a shot which eluded Clemence and ended in the Liverpool net.

The picture of Charlie lying on the pitch, his arms raised high after scoring, is one of the best-known images in English football. The length of his celebration was partly due to fatigue, but also because he was aware of time slipping by. No ref, no matter how hard-bitten, would risk his life by issuing a booking under such circumstances for time-wasting, and Charlie knew this: 'People say why did I lie on the floor after the goal. They said I was tired. But I think I was a lot cleverer than people thought.' Nevertheless, it was a splendidly executed and very important goal.

The final whistle sounded, and Arsenal had done it. This exhausted collection of 'no hopers' (in the eyes of most of the press) had just become only the second team in the 20th century to have won the 'Double', and they fully deserved the honour and the lengthy celebrations which ensued across Islington – an estimated half a million people gathered in the area around the Town Hall – and far beyond.

The 1970/71 FA Cup-winning team was: *Wilson, Rice, McNab, Storey (Kelly), McLintock, Simpson, Armstrong, Graham, Radford, Kennedy, George*

Above: Frank McLintock raises the FA Cup at Wembley. *Colorsport*

Left: Bertie Mee *(left)* and Liverpool's Bill Shankly *(right)*, lead their teams out at Wembley. *Alamy*

63

Arsenal: 1970/71 Double Heroes

In my opinion, the winning of the 1970/71 Double is the greatest single achievement in the history of Arsenal Football Club.

I am aware that such a statement relegates to a secondary status, at least in this respect, the achievements of several of the great managers (notably Chapman and Wenger) as well as players ranging from Alex James to Thierry Henry. However, what Bertie Mee, Don Howe and these particular players did that season was unparalleled, and the team deserves recognition, in several ways, as the greatest-ever Gunners side.

These players may not have been the most technically gifted nor blessed with the supreme talents of some of the most celebrated names in Arsenal's history. Indeed, some of this particular squad – which included a schoolmaster, a local ragamuffin or two, and younger players, alongside their older and more experienced but often unheralded colleagues – may even have struggled to earn first-team status in some of the wealthier, more grandiose clubs in the First Division.

The team also had to struggle against the generally negative perceptions of Arsenal in the world of English football. The 'grand' clubs of the day often shared a mild distaste for the Gunners and their 'arriviste' origins (although they were quick enough with their cheque-books when young talent was available at Highbury). The press and radio generally shared this bias, often repeating the mantra of 'boring Arsenal' while forgetting the unexpected, swift counter-attacks and the smartly-taken, unpredictable goals with which Arsenal silenced vocal opposing supporters.

The players, however, paid little attention to the media sniping, as they'd heard it all before. This class of 1970/71 was tougher than most, however, and they well knew what the club required of them. They set about proving themselves to a world which was intent on denigrating their ability. Their burgeoning abilities and successes quickly quietened the critics.

Their dedication, single-mindedness and durability, the lack of selfishness, the confidence in themselves and in their fellow players and, most importantly, the importance and respect they all felt was due to Arsenal Football Club, all marked them out as a unique footballing side. Bertie Mee spoke the truth about the Double side when he praised them, saying: 'technically there were certain deficiences, but our other qualities were superb'.

They won the Double with only 16 players which, even in those days of small squads, was a remarkable feat and bears witness to the players' determination and strength of will. Three of the team – Wilson, McLintock and Armstrong – played in every League game that season; Radford, Rice and Kennedy missed only one; and Storey and McNab had only two absences that season.

These players, Bertie Mee, Don Howe, the backroom staff and the club's loyal supporters that season collectively ensured that a selfless blend of leadership, talent, perseverance and adherence to a common aim had brought back a much-deserved triumph to the marble halls of Highbury.

64

What goes up must come down

In non-mathematical terms, Isaac Newton's Third Law of Motion states that for every action, there is an equal and opposite reaction. Or to put it in even simpler terms, this Third Law is what happened to Arsenal in the years following their Double triumph.

Between the Double and the late 1970s, virtually all the players who had formed that historic team had left Arsenal, and the club went into decline. Of course, players come and players go, but it is unusual for everyone to move on so quickly after such a triumphant experience. The first to leave was perhaps the most unexpected. In July 1971 Don Howe, the man who had helped so much to engineer the Double, was appointed manager of West Bromwich Albion. Amid mutterings of 'betrayal', Howe left the club, but he was only the first.

65

The slide begins

The following League season of 1971/72 saw an out-of-sorts, punch-drunk Arsenal eliminated from the League Cup by Sheffield United and then beaten 5-1 by Wolves, both in November.

But then (being Arsenal) they embarked on a 14-game unbeaten League run until March. They then wobbled again, and ended in fifth place in the League, one spot away from the next season's European qualification. This season, however, they had qualified for the major continental competition, the European Cup.

Having won their first two rounds by a total of 12 goals to one, Arsenal had the misfortune to meet Ajax in the quarter-final. Inspired by Johan Cruyff – and including the likes of Ruud Krol, Johan Neeskens, Arie Haan and Piet Keizer – Ajax were title holders (and about to claim the next two) and were virtually unbeatable.

In the first leg in Amsterdam, Kennedy had the effrontery to give the Gunners an early 1-0 lead but, despite heroics from Wilson and the defence, Ajax notched up two goals with no further reply. At Highbury, young Scottish hopeful Peter Marinello missed an excellent early opportunity, and Graham's headed own goal did not improve matters. Arsenal were out.

In that season's FA Cup, third and fourth round defeats of Swindon and Reading led to a three-game duel and eventual win over Derby. A goal from recent signing, England international midfielder Alan Ball – whose transfer fee of £220,000 from Everton set a League record – was sufficient for Arsenal to beat Orient, and another replay against Stoke was won in the semi-final by a Radford strike. A dour FA Cup Final, as they so often are, was won 1-0 by Leeds United.

So, in their first season after the Double, Arsenal won nothing, and there was a deflated, dispirited air around Highbury. The next few seasons would prove little different.

66

McLintock and Graham exit Highbury

In 1972/73 Arsenal were knocked out of the League Cup in November, and later in the season Second Division side Sunderland eliminated the team from the FA Cup at the semi-final stage. Although stuffed 5-0 by Derby in November, the Gunners were then unbeaten for 11 games, but they again lost their direction and ended in second place behind Liverpool: highly respectable, but no cigar.

The arrival of defender Jeff Blockley at the start of the season appeared to threaten Frank McLintock's position, and the long-standing captain and club inspiration left Highbury to join QPR in April 1973, with Ball assuming the club captaincy. Mee later admitted that bringing in Blockley, and thereby losing McLintock, had been his biggest managerial mistake. Before the following season was under way, George Graham had also taken his leave, this time for Manchester United. Confidence within Highbury was fast becoming a problem.

In 1973/74, Arsenal were kicked out of the League Cup by lowly Tranmere Rovers, beaten by Aston Villa in the FA Cup fourth round, and they won only 13 League games. They finished in tenth place, 20 points behind winners Leeds. At the conclusions of the following couple of seasons, Arsenal ended in, respectively, 16th and 17th, their lowest positions in the First Division for around 50 years.

In March 1976, Bertie Mee bowed to the inevitable and retired as manager of Arsenal. He had been highly respected at the club, but his age and his declining influence over the dressing room were now counting against him.

As for the Double team, Ray Kennedy went to Liverpool, Charlie George was off to Derby, Radford was West Ham-bound, McNab became a Wolves man, and so on. After the slightly later departures of Peter Storey and Pat Rice, they had all embraced pastures new. Wilson and Rice were to return, however, on the coaching side, while a significantly less diffident and more disciplined George Graham was to make his mark the following decade as manager of the club.

It was time for a new, younger manager, and for a rethink on the future of the club. After a few weeks of looking around and making discreet enquiries, the Arsenal board unveiled their choice as Arsenal's new manager.

67

Highbury: a brief personal digression

It was around this time – the mid-1970s – that I made my first visit to Highbury. I had recently moved from Edinburgh, secured a job in London as a publishing editor, and I lived a short bus ride from the stadium. When I was a kid I had been a rabid 'blue-nose', or Rangers supporter, and there seemed to be a similarity between the 'Gers and Arsenal, not least among fans of the game, in that both clubs were either loved or hated: there was little in between.

One of my new work colleagues, Doug, was a long-term Arsenal man, and we joined up at home games with a few of his mates on the Clock End. Two of the guys – Charlie and Phil – were born and brought up in a block of council flats adjoining the West Stand, and they had Arsenal in their blood. The rest of our small posse were also locals. From that day on, I rarely missed a game.

We would shout and sing our support for the 'Arse', howl down the opposition and their supporters, enjoy a half-time pint in the Clock End bar, and return for a second half of more good-humoured ranting. As the years passed, I would also stand on the North Bank or sit in the East Stand and watch the games, revelling in the footballing camaraderie, insults and jokes. Highbury became my second home, and I became a 'Gooner'.

The term 'Gooner' was gleefully adopted by Arsenal fans. The name supposedly derived from the coachloads of Scandinavian

Arsenal supporters – usually to be found on the North Bank – who travelled across the North Sea to 'The Home of Football' (as Chapman had christened the stadium), and they found it easier to pronounce the 'u' sound as 'oo'. The North Bank loved this, and so was born 'Ooo, ooo, ooo to be / Ooo to be a Gooner'. We all became 'Gooners'.

I loved that old stadium: its close proximity to the pitch, which was the smallest in the League; the four open corners, offering generous views of Muswell Hill, Blackstock Road and the outside world when little was happening on the pitch; the pre-match parade of the Police Metropolitan Band (particularly when the bandmaster dropped his baton at the North Bank); the Trodos ad at the foot of the West Stand assuring us that 'a meal without wine is like a day without sunshine'; the ever-unpredictable but always determined pace and movement of the Arsenal teams; the moments of brilliance displayed by such stellar players as Brady and Bergkamp; the little club shop run by Jack Kelsey beside the Clock End entrance on Avenell Road; the socialising and jocularity in the bars; the absence of unnecessarily violent behaviour, both organised and personal; and so much else. The quality of the football varied, though, but that's to be expected over so many years.

After the club moved in 2006 to Ashburton Grove, Highbury was converted into 'luxury accommodation', with a gym, swimming pool and all the rest of it. But every time I think about, or drive past, the old stadium, I do so with a warm sense of nostalgia and with deep affection.

68

Welcome to the hot seat, Tel

It was quite an achievement for the Arsenal board to pick such an entirely different personality to succeed the dapper, middle-aged and quintessentially English Bertie Mee, but they managed it.

In June 1976, 34-year-old, Northern Irish ex-international football captain Terry Neill took over as the youngest manager in the history of Arsenal Football Club. Not only that, but he was the first Arsenal manager ever to have been manager of the bad guys up the road: Tottenham Hotspur.

He was familiar with Highbury, however, as he had made 275 appearances for Arsenal, as a centre-half or left-half, mainly from the mid-1960s until 1970, when he was appointed player/manager at Hull City.

He seemed unhappy about managing his ex-teammates, so 1976/77 saw the departure of Kelly, Radford and Storey. The only Double players who remained were the dependable right-back Pat Rice, the attacking left-back Sammy Nelson and the popular winger Geordie Armstrong. Geordie was to leave in 1979. Alan Ball fell out with Neill, and was moved on to Southampton, with Rice becoming captain.

Neill was fortunate – or perhaps prescient – that several younger, promising players had been coming through from the youth team, none more welcome than Liam Brady, an exceptional, multi-talented left-half whose overall footballing awareness was soon to galvanise the team. Others included, in particular, the confident 18-year-old centre-half David O'Leary and the skilful, goalscoring Frank Stapleton, as well as Wilf Rostron, Trevor Ross, Paul Vaessen and Brian Hornsby.

In Neill's first season, Arsenal ended eighth in the League, which included a run of eight straight defeats, the worst in Arsenal's history. Neill commented after one of these defeats that 'we couldn't have beaten 11 dustbins on that display'. Arsenal were also knocked out at an early stage from both Cups.

From his previous club Spurs, Neill acquired the lanky, ginger-haired, Scottish centre-half Willie Young who, although frequently erratic with the ball, was an effective stopper. He quickly became a crowd favourite ('We've got the biggest Willie in the land'). Young partnered O'Leary in central defence, with Rice and Nelson as the full-backs. Neill also bought, for £333,333 from Newcastle United, Malcolm 'Supermac' Macdonald, a stocky but speedy English international centre-forward, who was top scorer during his two-year stay at Highbury. Maverick ball-player Alan Hudson also arrived, but his stay was a relatively brief one.

Over the summer of 1977 the taciturn Don Howe returned to Highbury as head coach, and his experience and emphasis on team discipline soon made him an essential foil to the more ebullient Neill. Alan Sunderland, a more than useful goal scorer, arrived from Wolves. Neill again raided Spurs for Steve Walford and, importantly, keeper Pat Jennings who was considered 'past it' by the imprudent Spurs management. At Arsenal, Jennings remained first-choice goalie for the following eight years, made over 300 appearances for the club and retired aged 39. Past it? I think Spurs miscalculated that one.

69

Two seasons and four Finals

Although Arsenal ended a respectable fifth in the League at the end of 1977/78, Neill seemed more of a 'knock-out' man, as evidenced by the club's reaching the semi-final of that season's League Cup, only to be beaten by Liverpool.

In that season's FA Cup, Macdonald and Stapleton joined up in attack, and scored the goals which eventually saw Arsenal face Ipswich in the Final. However, a combination of injuries, lack of fitness and sluggish play in the Arsenal team led to Ipswich winning the FA Cup by a solitary goal. The game marked the effective end of Macdonald's career due to injury, but he had scored a total of 55 goals for the club in his two years at Highbury. As for the result, the eternal optimist Neill stated 'we will be back next season, more determined than ever', and he was absolutely right.

Although Arsenal began 1978/79 in lacklustre fashion – including a shock early elimination from the League Cup by Rotherham United – by Christmas they had put together a ten-match undefeated run. Its culmination was a 5-0 defeat of Spurs at White Hart Lane, and the game's highlight was the stunning fifth goal, an unstoppable, curling, left-foot shot by Brady from the edge of the box. To this day, they still show this goal on TV.

They were also in the UEFA Cup, in which tournament they defeated Lokomotiv Leipzig, and Hajduk Split, until beaten in the third round by Red Star Belgrade. In the League they ended the season in seventh place.

70

A bum rap for Sammy

Sammy Nelson was one of the friendliest and most popular players at Highbury, with his teammates, staff and fans alike. A Northern Ireland international, he had joined the Gunners in 1966, came through the youth team, was the regular left-back, and his upfield surges, linking with Liam Brady, and his tackling had endeared him to the fans.

On 3 April 1979, during the first half of a League game against Coventry at Highbury, he deflected a Coventry shot into his own net. It was an obvious own goal and he was barracked, in a good-natured manner, mainly by a section of Arsenal fans in the North Bank. In the second half, Sammy made amends for his error by scoring the equaliser, not a skill for which he was noted. Perhaps still slightly riled, but probably just for a laugh, Sammy turned his back to the North Bank, bent down, dropped his shorts and 'mooned' the North Bank. The reaction was one of hilarity, and no one could have been offended.

Sammy's friendly little gesture – the equivalent of sticking out one's tongue at a friend – led to the club suspending him for two weeks and fining him two weeks' wages. The FA also reacted primly. The result? He became even more of a fans' favourite: 'Sammy, Sammy, show us yer bum . . .'

71

'The Five-Minute Final'

The third round of the FA Cup that season was a tiring process. Between January 6 and 22, Arsenal took five games to knock out Third Division Sheffield Wednesday. Attacking midfielder Brian Talbot arrived from Ipswich to add his presence to Arsenal's forwards, and he scored in the fourth-round defeat of Notts County. Next up was Nottingham Forest at the City Ground, where Forest had been unbeaten in 52 matches, but a Stapleton headed goal (a rare event) saw Arsenal through. They then disposed of Southampton and Wolves to reach, again, the FA Cup Final.

Their opponents were Manchester United on 12 May 1979. Brady, Stapleton and Talbot were outstanding. Brady, in particular, was having a splendid match along with young left-winger Graham Rix and, with five minutes left to play, Arsenal were cruising 2-0. However, Gordon McQueen and Sammy McIlroy pulled back two quick goals just before the end. Then Brady found Rix who floated in a cross which Sunderland nudged into the net, and the final whistle blew. Arsenal had won the FA Cup, and Brady had been unquestionably dominant.

The young Irishman announced after the game that he would be moving to Juventus at the end of the following season in order to gain a wider experience of the game. After Brady's display in the 'five-minute final', as this game became known, there were few who would begrudge him this opportunity.

72

. . . and two more Finals to go

Season 1979/80 is best remembered by Gooners for Arsenal's exploits in the Cups, although they ended the League season in a commendable fourth position. Stapleton and Sunderland each scored 14 League goals, and Sammy even picked up two (once you get in the habit . . .).

In the League Cup in early September, Arsenal recorded their highest-ever win in that tournament with a 7-0 wipe-out of once-'mighty' Leeds United at Highbury, Stapleton claiming a hat-trick. So how did they contrive to lose 4-3 away to Swindon Town (again) in the quarter-final in mid-December? It's a mystery.

The results were more favourable in the FA Cup until they met, in the semi-final, the League winners-to-be, Liverpool. In just over a fortnight in April, they played four matches against their Scouse rivals, a goal by Talbot squeezing Arsenal into their third FA Cup Final in a row, this time their opponents being Second Division West Ham United. Arsenal had played two League games in nine days since Talbot released them from Liverpool's clutches, and they were a tired side.

A rare headed goal by Trevor Brooking (who, to me, appeared to be falling over when the ball struck him) gave West Ham a 1-0 victory and the FA Cup. Meanwhile, Arsenal had just four more days to prepare for only their second European Final, this one being on 14 May 1980 against Valencia in the Cup Winners' Cup in the Heysel Stadium, Brussels.

Arsenal had seen off Fenerbahce, Magdeburg and IFK Goteborg, and even 'La Vecchia Signora' of Italian football, Juventus, in the two-legged semi-final in April. Juve had taken a 1-1 Highbury draw back to Turin and their forbidding stadium where no British team had ever achieved a victory. With two minutes remaining of a goalless draw, young substitute Paul Vaessen scored the winner and achieved his moment of glory.

The Final on 14 May 1980 was an unexciting and goal-free affair which went to penalties. Mario Kempes and Liam Brady missed the first two attempts, everyone else, excepting Graham Rix, converted, and Valencia won the trophy. The game is sometimes referred to as 'Rix's miss'. Rix was inconsolable but people usually forget Brady's miss (one of the advantages, perhaps, of being 'a legend').

73

Four Finals . . . and one trophy

Arsenal had played 15 matches in 45 days and, over that season, they had contested a total of 70 top-level games, a number which no previous British team had ever undertaken. It is little surprise that the players were exhausted. In the summer of 1980, playmaker Liam Brady moved to Juventus and, as he had given one year's notice, this was deemed honourable. Stapleton's departure to Manchester United in 1981, however, was regarded by many Gooners as 'disloyal', as the striker discovered when he and his new club visited Highbury.

Again, Arsenal entered into a relatively fallow period, but one with little evidence of impending improvement. Although for the following three seasons Arsenal remained in the top ten of the League – which from 1981/82 allocated three points for a win and one for a draw – they did little of consequence in Europe. In 1982/83 they reached the semi-final of both Cups but were eliminated in each case by Manchester United, but they achieved little else. The team appeared to have lost its way, with players coming and going from other clubs and, with rare exceptions, within the youth team, and a noticeable decline in crowd attendance at Highbury underlined the fans' disenchantment.

Neill had acquired in 1980 the small, speedy left-back Kenny Sansom from Crystal Palace to replace Sammy Nelson, who soon left, and in 1981/82 the purchase of central defender Chris

Whyte spelt the end for Willie Young. The following season striker Tony Woodcock arrived from Koln. Lee Chapman ('the biggest transfer mistake of my career', said Neill) and Vladimir Petrovic also signed up for the Gunners, but neither player remained for long at Highbury. Sansom was to become club captain, and Woodcock demonstrated his scoring ability, but Arsenal were winning nothing.

Chairman Peter Hill-Wood handed Neill a new, improved contract in 1983, but pressure was building up for a change of direction and perhaps leadership for Arsenal. The fans were unhappy, and there was also uncertainty and disagreement at Arsenal's board level. In 1983 a wealthy, 36-year-old commodity broker and businessman named David Dein had become a director. Dein had long been an Arsenal supporter, and he was one of the first at a senior level in the English game to understand the longer-term commercial potential of both Arsenal and English football as a whole. Dein's vision for the future of the club was to become increasingly influential over the following few years.

In the summer of 1983 Neill bought Celtic's top scorer Charlie Nicholas for £650,000 but, by late November of that season, their home League Cup knock-out by Walsall – 50 years after their deeply embarrassing defeat by the same club – Nicholas had managed only a meagre handful of goals. The chairman, Peter Hill-Wood, and his board knew what had to be done.

As Neill ruefully related: 'Peter Hill-Wood said "I suppose you know why you're here?" I thought to myself, "I know I'm Irish but I'm not that dumb".' Neill, whose main problem had been his inability to replace Brady and Stapleton, resigned as Arsenal's manager, and in mid-December 1983 head coach Don Howe took over the role. There seemed little Howe could do to bring back the winning habit to the club, other than try to raise the 'goals for' column by taking on England striker Paul Mariner. After the events of this season, sixth place in the League was a minor triumph.

In Pat Jennings' final season before retiring – 1984/85 – Howe brought in replacement keeper John Lukic and right-back Viv Anderson, the first black English international footballer. This was all very well, but the team was not scoring enough goals. They were then humiliated in the FA Cup – knocked out by Fourth Division York City – and defeated by Oxford United in the League Cup.

By March 1986, regular attendances at Highbury had fallen to under 20,000, and Arsenal exited the FA Cup after a fifth round replay in which they lost to Luton Town. They did beat Coventry City 3-0 in a League match towards the end of that month, but Howe resigned after the game. He was supposedly angry at rumours that Terry Venables had been offered the Arsenal manager's job behind his back, but it did appear to many that Howe had jumped before he was finally pushed.

74

George Graham arrives back

In May 1986, the besuited, 41-year-old Scotsman who strode up the wide steps on Avenell Road into the 'Marble Halls' of Highbury Stadium looked remarkably familiar. He was pretty much identical to the younger man who, 14 years previously, had casually sauntered down the same steps, Double medal in his pocket, on his way to Manchester United.

However, the recent arrival projected an air of steely determination and purpose, both of which had appeared absent in the younger lad. Or perhaps these traits had been nascent in the departee? Then, 'Stroller' George had left Highbury for Manchester United. Now, George Graham had returned as manager of Arsenal Football Club. Age and experience – his previous role had been manager of Millwall – had changed George's outlook on the world of football and, as he made his way to his office, the new manager reflected on the recent upheavals in the club.

George didn't mess about. His two international forwards – Tony Woodcock and Paul Mariner – were both out of contract and left the club. Unusually, one might suppose, although his playing position was attacking midfield, George made defence his first priority on the pitch, then he concentrated on developing young players throughout the team.

In goal remained the dependable John Lukic. His defence was Anderson, Tony Adams (who was centre-half in every game in 1986/87), O'Leary and Sansom. The midfield comprised the speedy, attack-minded David Rocastle, Steve Williams, stylish Paul Davis and Martin Hayes, while up front was 20-year-old Niall Quinn alongside Charlie Nicholas. Winger Perry Groves ('El Pel') arrived from Colchester and, again unusually for a new manager, was the only early signing. They soon overcame a dodgy start to 1986/87, and by the end of January Graham's side topped the League table.

Between their away defeats by Nottingham Forest in late September and Manchester United in late January, Arsenal's young side were undefeated in 22 games. That Graham's tactics were essentially defensive is revealed by his team scoring 47 goals over that period while conceding only 11.

Graham was imposing a greater sense of discipline, on and off the pitch, and his plan was to discard the older, established players and to replace them with promising members of the youth team and also importing like-minded individuals from elsewhere. In one of his early team talks he revealed his attitude to the older squad by telling them they could, by mistake and once only, call him 'George', but thereafter he was to be addressed as 'boss'.

The club's 'centenary' game was celebrated on 23 December 1986, appropriately when Arsenal were leading the League. Played at Highbury, the opposition was Southampton in a League game which Arsenal won 1-0, scored by the 6ft 5in, 19-year-old forward Niall Quinn. A crowd of over 38,000 crammed into the ground to celebrate the occasion. The Master of Ceremonies was Double keeper Bob Wilson, and among the many renowned ex-players who attended were Ted Drake, Joe Mercer and George Male, who was the only attendee to have played under Herbert Chapman.

After their Manchester United defeat, Arsenal typically entered a run of nine League games without a win and, despite a resurgence later in the season, they completed 1986/87 in fourth place. They were also out of the FA Cup at the quarter-final stage by losing 1-3 to Watford at Highbury.

75

A trophy, after eight years

Ten days before they were done over by Watford in the FA Cup, Arsenal had already qualified for the League Cup Final, but the semi-final had been a gruelling, three-match struggle against Spurs. The old enemy won the first leg at Highbury by a single goal. Gus Caesar had replaced the injured Anderson, but he was ineffective against Chris Waddle and was subbed by young Michael Thomas. The game was Thomas's first experience at a senior level.

In the second leg at the Lane, a Lukic mistake gave Spurs an aggregate 2-0 lead at half-time. The Spurs PA system, or propaganda unit, then broadcast that Arsenal were finished and told Spurs fans where to buy tickets for the Final. This was badly misjudged and condescending, and an attitude which angered and revitalised the Arsenal players. By the middle of the second half Arsenal had scored twice, and the score ended level on aggregate.

Three days later, again at the Lane (location decided by a coin toss) but with over 10,000 Arsenal fans in the crowd, Spurs took the lead but, with eight minutes left, Ian Allinson, on for an injured Nicholas, equalised. In injury time, Rocastle scored the winner, and Arsenal were in the Final. An Arsenal fanzine – *One-Nil Down, Two-One Up* – was named in honour of this game, regarded as a heroic performance by the Highbury boys.

By comparison, the Final on 5 April 1987 against Liverpool was relatively uneventful, until near the end. Liverpool were clear favourites and Rush, as usual, scored in the first half. Just on half-time, Nicholas bundled in an equaliser and the score was level. With seven minutes left to play, substitute Groves sped down the wing and crossed to Nicholas, whose mishit deceived both him and keeper Ray Clemence, but entered the net.

Arsenal won 2-1, and George Graham had won a trophy – Arsenal's first in eight years – in his first season as Arsenal manager.

The team celebrate their League Cup Final win over Liverpool at Wembley. *Colorsport*

76

George has another go

Much encouraged by the energetic commitment of his young side, George made more changes. This season –1987/88 – was a comparative let-down, although he did get rid off the latest North Bank hero, 'Bonnie Prince' Charlie Nicholas, who played the first three games, was dropped, and was sold to Aberdeen in January. In came tall, intelligent centre-forward Alan Smith, aggressive midfielder Kevin Richardson and buzzing little left-back Nigel Winterburn, while Viv Anderson left for Manchester United.

In the early part of the season Arsenal won ten games in succession – during which a young Paul Merson made his first senior appearance – but, after a 0-1 home defeat by Southampton in November, they managed only one more win in the following 11 games, and they finished the season in sixth spot. In the FA Cup they surrendered to Nottingham Forest at Highbury in the quarter-final.

So, it was the League Cup again, and Arsenal almost won it. They battled their way to Wembley for the Final against Luton Town on 24 April and it was a close thing. However, Winterburn missed a penalty, and another error by Gus Caesar in the final minutes allowed Luton to score the winner, beating Arsenal 3-2.

Although it was clear that Arsenal's main problem was goalscoring (lack of), over the summer of 1988 George offloaded ex-captain Sansom and bought in two defenders: pacy right-back Lee Dixon (to replace Anderson) and hard-tackling Steve Bould (another centre-back). Winterburn took over the left-back role from Sansom. Graham also acquired a left-winger, Brian Marwood.

Alan Smith was an agile centre-forward with a well-developed positional sense and a powerful shot. Rocastle and Thomas were tricky, attacking midfielders, and Merson was an inside-forward, and often a left-winger who cut inside and shot, in the manner of Bastin. And full-backs Dixon and Winterburn were both attack-inclined.

Although Marwood also became a regular team member and accurate ball supplier, the long-ball philosophy depended essentially on Smith's ability to control, distribute or convert. The scoring opportunities of Quinn and Hayes were minimised (Hayes scored 19 League goals in George's opening season, and only one during the following season). Nominally described as 'counter-attack', the system led to the tag of 'boring Arsenal' again being heard from the terraces.

'Boring' or not, Arsenal were eliminated at an early stage in both cups and, although ignominious as this appeared, it did mean that they could now concentrate on the League. By the end of January they led the First Division, 19 points ahead of Liverpool. However, Liverpool were beginning a 24-game undefeated run and, as Arsenal lost points, the gap between the clubs gradually narrowed.

In mid-March Graham tried out a 5-2-3 formation, with O'Leary acting as sweeper, Rocastle moving forward and the full-backs encouraged to press forward when possible, and this new system brought immediate results. As the balding Bould later said: 'I lost my barnet flicking the ball on for all them years from the near post from Brian Marwood's corners'. However, after the Hillsborough Disaster on 15 April they stopped playing for 16 days, only to come back on May Day with a 5-0 crushing of Norwich. Smith was on top form, and Norwich manager Dave Stringer said: 'We were outclassed and outplayed. It was a hammering.'

Other results, however, did not all go Arsenal's way, and before the final game of the season Liverpool's surge had led them to the top of the League, two points ahead of the Gunners. Arsenal's final game was on the evening of 26 May 1989 at Anfield, and to lift the League title they had to win 2-0.

77

'It's up for grabs now . . .'

The *Daily Mirror* gave them a glimmer of hope ('Arsenal's championship is now all but over') while the *Daily Mail* ('Arsenal do not have a prayer') was more emphatic and agreed with the major bookies who were quoting odds of 7-1 against Arsenal beating Liverpool by two goals to nil that evening. No one in the media or the world of football gave Arsenal a chance. But in the dressing room Graham had said to his team: 'Go out and play without fear because you've got nothing to lose.' So that's what they did.

At half-time the score remained nil-nil, with both teams spurning chances. A few minutes after the interval, Winterburn sent in an indirect free-kick and Smith headed the ball into the net. Despite Liverpool players claiming he hadn't touched it, the goal was given. 1-0. Arsenal kept up the pressure but by injury time the score remained 1-0.

With the Kop End chanting 'Champions', Lukic threw the ball to a surprised Dixon, who was expecting a punt upfield from the keeper, but the right-back swiftly passed a long ball to Smith, who in turn found Thomas in space on the right. Thomas ran forward with the ball at his feet, tried to lob Nicol, the ball rebounded and Thomas kept going, pursued frantically by Liverpool defenders.

TV commentator Brian Moore, caught up in the emotion of Thomas's last-gasp attempt, told his millions of viewers 'It's up for grabs now . . .' as Bruce Grobbelaar came out of his goal towards the advancing Thomas.

Still keeping his nerve, Thomas flicked the ball over the keeper and into the net, and the scorer somersaulted away in a delighted celebration. The final whistle blew, and Arsenal had done it: 2-0 in the last seconds and they had won the League title. It was one of the most astonishing endings to a football match which I have ever witnessed.

Michael Thomas scores his title-winning goal in the last minute of the final game of the season, past Steve Nicol and goalkeeper Bruce Grobbelaar, at Anfield. *Colorsport*

78

Getting over it all

After the exertion and determination displayed by his squad over the previous three seasons, at the start of 1989/90 Graham showed his confidence in the players by buying only Icelandic midfielder Siggi Jonsson.

Although they had won the League, the post-Heysel ban on English clubs remained in force, so there was no entry into the European Cup. Nor did they remain long in the other knock-outs, going down in the League Cup in November to Oldham Athletic and in the FA Cup in January to QPR. They were doing better in the League and were leading the table by mid-December. On 4 November at Highbury, David O'Leary had made his 622nd appearance for Arsenal, overtaking Geordie Armstrong's appearance record. During that game – a 4-3 win against Norwich – O'Leary ironically scored his first League goal for six years.

The rest of that season was pretty much up and down for the Gunners, and they ended in fourth position, respectable enough although a distant 17 points behind winners Liverpool. Again, the defence was mainly responsible for the top-four ranking, keeping 14 clean sheets in the League, while the top scorer was Smith with a disappointing ten goals. Scoring goals remained difficult for this Arsenal team. However, towards the season's end, Kevin Campbell, a tough, bustling striker, was making noticeable progress.

79

Time to get moving again

The 'boss' – or 'Gaddafi' as he was becoming known by some of his more disgruntled squad – was aware that his team needed to score more goals.

In came lightning-fast, goalscoring winger Anders Limpar. Limpar's role was to create chances for Smith, the increasingly confident Merson and new attacker Campbell, while picking up a few himself. Centre-back Andy Linighan arrived to provide even more cover for the important defenders. And David Seaman came to Highbury for a record goalkeeper transfer fee of £1.3 million. Lukic left the club soon afterwards.

Looking back at Arsenal's 1990/91 season, Tony Adams commented 'there was a freshness to us from the outset', and so it proved. Beginning with their first game in late-August 1990, the Gunners did not lose in the League until they were narrowly beaten 2-1 by Chelsea on 2 February, a run of 17 games without defeat. This included the Old Trafford contest on 20 October when Winterburn clattered into Brian McClair, and the Scotsman not unnaturally retaliated, a confrontation which led to 21 players (Seaman keeping a discreet distance) indulging in an on-pitch barney. Limpar scored the only goal, but the following month saw an FA punishment of £50,000 for both clubs and, more painfully, a two-point deduction for Arsenal for their part in the 'Battle of Old Trafford'. Liverpool were now eight points clear.

Retaliation for Winterburn's late 'tackle' came on 28 November at Highbury when Arsenal were thrashed 6-2 by United in the League Cup. The blameless Seaman had let in a total of only six goals since the season began. The captain Tony Adams was shortly after sentenced to four months for drink driving, which upset things a bit. Arsenal backed Adams, who refused to sell his story to a slavering media, and he was released on 27 February to thunderous cheers, in time to captain the Gunners to a fifth round FA Cup win, achieved after a four-game slug-out with Leeds in the previous round, over Shrewsbury Town.

Any hopes of Arsenal again achieving the Double evaporated at Wembley in the FA Cup semi-final in mid-April, the first time the semi-final had ever occurred at the old stadium. A stunning free-kick in the fifth minute from Gazza, and two goals from Lineker, saw to that.

80

'Sit down, Dalglish . . .'

However, the previous month's win over Liverpool, thanks to Merson, kept the title challenge alive. I vividly recall standing in the Clock End in early December that season during the Scousers' earlier defeat (3-0), witnessing their manager Kenny Dalglish's constant jumping and screaming from his seat at the bottom of the East Stand, and my joining in the gleeful Gunner chants of 'Sit down, Dalglish'. By February he'd gone, soon to be replaced by 'hard man' Graeme Souness.

Nevertheless, it remained an extremely tight race for the League title. On 4 May Arsenal could only stutter to a 0-0 home draw with Sunderland, but on the same day Chelsea recorded a 4-2 win over the challenger. There were two games remaining and a gap of four points separated the two teams. The penultimate games were critical. If Liverpool lost to Forest, Arsenal had won the League.

And that's what happened. By a neat quirk of TV broadcasting, on 6 May the Arsenal game against Manchester United was to kick off at 8pm, after the Liverpool game had ended. Clough's men beat Liverpool at the City Ground, and George had claimed his second League title.

North London – or half of it – went into celebratory meltdown. That evening 40,000 fans at Highbury cheered on a rampant Arsenal as they swept United aside 3-1, Smith claiming a much-deserved hat-trick to bring his League total to 22 goals. Merson,

Limpar and Campbell between them had amassed 33, and the defence had conceded less than half of those let in by any other First Division side. It had been a tumultuous season, but they'd done it again.

George Graham, left, with his Barclays Manager of the Year trophy, and captain Tony Adams, with the Football League championship trophy, during the open-top bus parade to celebrate the side's league title win. *Colorsport*

81

'Ian Wright, Wright, Wright . . .'

Again, an Arsenal season which followed the gaining of a trophy turned out to be a frustrating combination of inspiration and humiliation. George's sixth year in charge followed this pattern, and it was a season of two halves.

For the first few months, it was the defence's turn to look shaky. Bould was injured, O'Leary was slowing down, Linighan and his stand-in deputy Colin Pates were unpredictable, Dixon was unreliable and, as a result, Seaman was nervous. In midfield, Rocastle was doing his best but Davis was dropped early in the season and replaced by young David Hillier, and Michael Thomas, the hero of 1989 at Anfield, was sold (to Liverpool, of all places) in December, partly because he had had enough of George's domineering attitude.

The attack was in fine spirits, however, particularly when another proven scorer, Ian Wright, joined for £2.5 million. 'Wrighty' immediately proved his worth by scoring a hat-trick on his League debut, and his name was thereafter rarely off the score sheet. He was, however, ineligible for Europe. The Heysel ban had been lifted, and Arsenal was the first English club since 1985 to re-enter the European Cup, a competition which Arsenal had last encountered 20 years previously.

In round one, Smith scored four times in the home defeat of Austria Memphis as they wrapped up a 6-2 aggregate win in

Ian Wright scores the first of his three goals on his League debut for Arsenal as Richard Hall of Southampton can only watch. *Colorsport*

Vienna. In the second round on 23 October, in front of 85,000 Portuguese in Benfica's magnificent Lisbon stadium, Arsenal survived the first leg 1-1 when Campbell equalised. At Highbury, Pates scored early on, but Benfica's ace Brazilian striker Isaias levelled with an unstoppable 30-yard volley. In injury time, Kulkov and Isaias made it 3-1 on the night, and out of Europe went Arsenal. A week before, they had been beaten by Coventry in the League Cup. So, by early November 1991, they were already out of two tournaments.

By 4 January 1992 they were out of three tournaments, after an FA Cup third round away game which Graham described, as well he might, as 'the lowest point of my career'. Self-deprecation was not normally one of George's strengths, but he showed it after this abysmal performance. Wrexham, who ended the previous season in 92nd place in the League, were the opponents. Arsenal were 1-0 ahead and apparently coasting, until Mickey Thomas hammered home a 30-yard free-kick which was closely followed by a Steve Watkins winner.

This left only the League as the Arsenal target. As reigning champions, they had an unimpressive start in which they won only two of their first seven games. In the seventh – against Coventry at Highbury on 7 September – Dixon took only two minutes to score, with a 30-yard lob. The problem was that the lob was over his own keeper, Seaman, who was desperately trying but failing to reach the ball. I missed it, as I was demonstrating my golf swing to my mate, unaware that the game had kicked off. Coventry won 2-1, but Arsenal won the following four matches. They had another hard time over Christmas. At the end of January they set off (at last) on a 17-game unbeaten run but, despite a pick-up in their scoring prowess, it was too late. As the season ended, Arsenal were in fourth spot.

The final game of that season, though, was a sad affair. At Highbury, another Wright hat-trick (his 24th League goal in 30 games) had contributed to a 5-1 dismissal of Southampton, but it was the old North Bank's last appearance. It was to be pulled down to make room for a new 12,500 seater stand, opening for 1993/94. I watched as several thousand Gooners staged a sit-down on the terracing, repeatedly chanting 'You'll never take the North Bank'.

It was, of course, futile, and the protestors gradually dwindled away, but I'd stood on that terracing often enough to realise that we were saying farewell to an integral part of Arsenal's history. Tears were even beginning to form in my eyes, but I cheered up by the time I arrived at the Bank of Friendship pub.

82

The Premier League

The Football Association's Premier League began in season 1992/93. A mural was erected on the North Bank to hide the building works, and it stretched 75 yards wide and 18 yards high. The thousands of faces which were painted on was an attempt to simulate a large, cheerful crowd. It was hastily repainted when a player mentioned to 'the boss' that there were no black spectators represented anywhere on this giant artwork. The absence of real people limited crowd capacity to 29,000 at Highbury for this season.

David Rocastle had moved on to Leeds, and midfielder John Jensen came in from Brondby as a replacement. Martin Keown, who had fallen out over payment with Graham in 1986, came back in February to add his intelligent distribution and man-marking skills to the ever-expanding Arsenal back line.

Whatever the reason – Graham's increasing fondness for a strong defence did not help – the Gunners suffered their worst League performance for ten years. They began well, winning five of their first seven games, but things started to go awry. In December they improved, but they then won only five games between the end of January and the end of term. They finished the season in tenth place. They also scored fewer goals than any other club in the new League, and they won only 15 of their 42 games.

However, as has frequently been the case with Arsenal, success in the cups often has little in common with League progress. This season both Finals were against the same club, Sheffield Wednesday.

In the League Cup Final on 18 April, Sheffield scored first and Merson equalised. Merse then crossed the ball for the winning goal, scored by the otherwise unheralded Steven Morrow. Arsenal won the Cup 2-1. After the game, Tony Adams lifted up Morrow onto his shoulders, and then accidentally dropped him. Morrow broke his arm when he hit the ground, and Adams was deeply upset at his own over-exuberant clumsiness.

The FA Cup Final on 20 May was, thankfully, a less celebratory affair. After a fairly dull game which went into extra time at 1-1, a replay was called for the following Tuesday. This replay also dragged on until extra time, when the rugged figure of Andy Linighan rose like a swan to head in a corner from the excellent Merson, and Andy scored the winning goal. Neither game was a classic, but it did mean that Arsenal became the first club in the history of English football to hold both the League Cup and the FA Cup in the same season.

83

Watch out, George

There it stood, the new North Bank, gazing magnanimously at its now visibly ageing neighbours. The Clock End, too, was soon about to reveal its all-seater status. People were now able to sit down all round Highbury, and stand up only to celebrate the many moments of excitement. The 1993/94 season was an opportune time to test these new seats, as little of interest was happening on the pitch. However, Highbury was now probably the most attractive football stadium in the country.

The League was disappointing. Wright was in his normally frisky mood in front of goal (top scorer with 23) but Campbell, Merson and Smith seemed disinterested. Limpar fell out with George, was dropped early in the season, played seven more games, and was sold to Everton in March. As George remarked, 'Anders and I never got on the same wavelength'.

The team were unpredictable and, when they won only three of their last ten games, they were perhaps fortunate to finish in fourth place, albeit 21 points behind Manchester United. They were also knocked out early from both cups.

Graham was obsessed about winning in Europe. In the Cup Winners' Cup, Arsenal, 3-0 ahead after Highbury, achieved an astonishing 7-0 destruction of Standard Liege in Belgium, a scoreline which again demonstrated their unpredictability. Likewise, coming away with an aggregate 1-0 quarter-final victory over Torino was unexpected.

In the semi-final in Paris against PSG – Ginola, Weah et al – Wright scored for a 1-0 first-half lead. At half-time, the PA played the Pet Shop Boys' 'Go West', a tune which the Gooners in the crowd adopted and re-sung as 'One-nil to the Arsenal'. It quickly became one of the most popular chants in the North Bank repertoire.

Back for the second leg at Highbury, Campbell headed in a Dixon cross for an aggregate 2-1 lead. Wright then launched into a violent tackle, and realised he'd already had a booking and that he'd miss the Final. He went off in tears, the score remained 1-0 and Arsenal were in the Final.

On 4 May in Copenhagen they met Parma in the Final. Arsenal were unchanged against, in anyone's eyes, a superior side, with Zola, Asprilla and Brolin outstanding players. In the 20th minute a ball from Dixon to Merson was intercepted and it fell to Smith who chested it down and, on the volley with his left foot, blasted it into the net. Arsenal held on grimly to the lead, and they won the game 1-0 and the Cup Winners' Cup.

84

George, you've been caught

The following season, however, wasn't Arsenal's best or most edifying. In the domestic cups they were knocked out by Liverpool (quarter-final, League Cup) and Millwall (third round, FA Cup). In the League they won three out of 17 games between late-October and mid-February, and three of their last ten games. Arsenal were fortunate to end this unhappy season in 12th place in the League.

On 31 December, Jensen finally scored a goal (against QPR in a 3-1 defeat for Arsenal). This was his first goal in 98 games for the Gunners, and T-shirts saying 'I saw Jensen score' were suddenly everywhere. Paul Merson probably didn't buy one, though, as he had earlier that autumn gone public with his admission that he was addicted to alcohol and cocaine. As had happened previously with Tony Adams, the club supported a tearful and deeply upset Merse, and he remained in rehabilitation until February.

The big story for George Graham, Arsenal and English football broke in December in the *Mail on Sunday*. The paper accused Graham of taking 'bungs' to the value of £425,000 from agent Rune Hauge in connection with transfer arrangements. Graham protested and claimed the payments were unsolicited. George Graham was sacked as manager of Arsenal on 21 February 1995, and Stewart Houston, known as 'Coneman' for his work at the London Colney training ground, was named as caretaker manager.

How, then, did George persuade Arsenal to sanction the arrival of three new players just days before they dismissed him? These newcomers were goal-scoring forwards Chris Kiwomya and John Hartson, and winger Glen Helder. On the very day George was fired, Helder made his Arsenal debut in a home League game against Forest. I was at the game and, like everyone around me, I thought he was outstanding, but he never lived up to that first appearance. Kiwomya also played, and scored the only goal. Both he and Hartson, in particular, scored useful goals for the team. However, they hung around, playing the occasional game, and they all soon left the club. Collectively, they had become known in the North Bank as 'George's Revenge'.

Earlier in the season, Arsenal had swamped Omonia Nicosia and narrowly squeezed past Brondby in the Cup Winners' Cup. In March, a Campbell goal in France in the quarter-final against Auxerre gave them an aggregate 2-1 win and a semi-final against Sven-Goran Eriksson's Sampdoria.

At Highbury in early April, and with an understrength team, Arsenal scored twice in three first-half minutes through Bould (twice his previous season's haul). Merson added a third for a 3-2 win to take to Italy. In a fast-moving contest in Genoa, an 87th-minute Schwarz free-kick equalised at 5-5. Extra time came and went, and then penalties became the decider. Seaman was heroic, brilliantly saved three penalties, and Arsenal were to meet Real Zaragoza in the Paris Final on 10 May.

The Final was a fairly tame affair, and was goalless until late in the second half when Zaragoza and then Hartson scored. It stayed at 1-1 until, in the last few seconds of extra time, Zaragoza's Nayim (ex-Spurs) spotted Seaman off his line, sent in a speculative lob from over 50 yards, and Seaman was stranded. One-two, the whistle blows and Arsenal have lost.

Since then, Spurs supporters at Arsenal games have needed little encouragement to start chanting 'Nayim, from the halfway line . . .' It can get very irritating.

85

Bruce Rioch comes and goes

In mid-June 1995, Bruce Rioch, Scotland ex-captain and most recently a successful manager at Bolton, was appointed manager of Arsenal. Like Graham, he was a disciplinarian but his view on how to play the game was quite different. George had increasingly urged the importance of defence and the long ball, while Rioch was a devotee of the passing game.

As an example, I was occasionally invited to the East Stand Upper Tier by a season-ticket-holder mate. Under George, I could follow much of the game by looking straight ahead, as the ball was normally in the air. Under Rioch, I had to look down, as the players were now passing to each other on the pitch. The latter was certainly more interesting.

Rioch believed in elegant, attacking football, and he was an advocate of the 3-5-2 system played, as often as possible, on the ground. Older players – including 'Smudger' Smith (345 appearances and 115 goals) and Kevin Campbell – were retiring or leaving, and younger players (Paul Dickov, Scott Marshall) were coming through.

The arrival of two particular players in the summer of 1995 signified that the days of 'boring Arsenal' had come to an end. David Platt, from Sampdoria for £4.75 million, was reigning England captain, with 62 caps, and was an attacking midfielder with a flair for scoring crucial goals. Dennis Bergkamp was a forward of international renown, with exceptional touch and technique, devastating goalscoring ability and, well, a footballing genius.

David Dein had enticed him from Inter Milan, where Bergkamp was unhappy, and Dein had placated Inter by shattering the Arsenal transfer record and paying them £7.5 million for the Dutchman. At last, Arsenal were spending money on world-class players, and few were as world-class as Dennis.

I was told by a Highbury insider that, on his first day of training, Bergkamp was surprised at the softness of the players' passing technique. He asked that they passed the ball to him with speed and power. Footballers can be a cynical bunch, so some of the team thought 'Right, I'll show him' and belted the ball to him as hard as they could. No matter the speed or angle of their delivery, Dennis controlled every ball which came his way, and he quickly passed it on. Thereafter, the Arsenal squad accepted him as an exceptional player and a valuable team member.

The 1995/96 season, though, was pretty much average. Arsenal were out of both cups – the League Cup at the semi-final and the FA Cup in the opening round – and they ended in fifth position in the League. It did seem that Rioch was a man slightly out of his depth and, as Merson said, 'he couldn't handle big-time players'. Seaman also commented that 'there was a bad atmosphere between Rioch and some of the players'. Wright was particularly unhappy and submitted a transfer request, but nonetheless he was again top scorer that season.

For me, the season's highlight was the 23 September League game in 1995 at Highbury against Southampton. It was a warm day, my son and I were sitting directly behind the North Bank goal, and Arsenal had played six League games: three wins, three draws. However, Bergkamp hadn't yet scored, and there was a growing number of Arsenal fans chanting 'what a waste of money'.

In this game, Bergkamp permanently silenced the doubters. During the first half, the Dutchman scored a magnificent volley into the Clock End goal from around 15 yards. You could probably have heard the roar in Woolwich. In the second half, he bemused, confused and twisted his way through what seemed the entire Southampton defence before unleashing an unstoppable shot from 20 yards into the top of the net. The North Bank went crazy, and with every justification.

In his autobiography, Dennis stresses the importance he placed on these goals, particularly the second one. As he recalls, 'certainly, from that day everything changed'.

86

Who is this French guy, anyway?

On 12 August 1996, Arsenal fired Rioch who, with a tenure of 14 months, became the shortest-serving manager in the club's history. While many sympathised with Rioch, speculation was intense as to his successor. Although Johan Cruyff had been spotted entering the Marble Halls the previous month, there was no truth in the rumours which this visit encouraged.

On 22 September, the club announced that Arsene Wenger, an urbane, multilingual Frenchman, most recently with Grampus Eight and Monaco, was the new manager. Although unknown to most supporters, Wenger over the next few years was to revolutionise the club.

Over that summer Jensen returned to Brondby and Stewart Houston later became manager of QPR. Two French midfielders – Remi Garde and Patrick Vieira – were enlisted, both at Wenger's suggestion, and Liam Brady returned as head of youth development at Highbury.

Wenger took over as manager on 12 October for the 2-0 away win at Blackburn. He'd been overseeing his innovations at London Colney – a new fitness regime and exercising, changed dietary habits, providing players with tactical insights and emphasising the importance of the passing game, and more, all in an attempt to add stamina and power to their natural talents. As a result, Tony Adams was encouraged to go public with his

Arsene Wenger reads the *Gunners* magazine after being appointed the club's new manager. *Colorsport*

'alcoholism', and his teammates were impressed with his honesty. Wright commented in praise of Tony, 'it took an awful lot of bottle' (although Wrighty could perhaps have chosen his words more carefully). In general, they shared Merson's view that 'the new manager has given us unbelievable belief' (we know what you mean, Merse, but . . .).

Perhaps so, but it took the players and Wenger time to get used to this season of change. They were defeated 6-4 in the UEFA Cup by Borussia Moenchengladbach, went out of the FA Cup fourth round 1-0 at the hands of Leeds, were kicked out of the League Cup 4-2 by Liverpool, and they ended third in the League. This League placing, however, guaranteed Arsenal a place in the UEFA Cup the following season.

A surprise at the beginning of 1997/98 was the departure of a Highbury favourite, Paul Merson, still only 29 years old, to Middlesbrough. Several others left, including Kiwomya and Helder. With Hartson having gone in February before the arrival of 17-year-old striker Nicolas Anelka from Monaco, 'George's Revenge' was no more.

Also from Monaco came French midfielder Emmanuel Petit, utility man Gilles Grimandi and forward Christopher Wreh, while winger Marc Overmars arrived for £5 million from Ajax. There were more newcomers this season, including young Austrian keeper Alex Manninger, Portuguese winger Luis Boa Morte and teenage defender Matthew Upson from Luton. With all this talent, and last season's glittering input, Wenger's Arsenal was nicely coming together, as this season would prove.

Arsenal were unexpectedly knocked out of the UEFA Cup by PAOK Salonika, but were unbeaten in the League until Derby defeated them in early November. During the run, a 3-3 draw with Leicester produced a hat-trick from Bergkamp, which were the top three goals on BBC TV's 'Goal of the Month' for August. Also, Wright became Arsenal's all-time highest goalscorer with his hat-trick in the mid-September Bolton game.

A 3-2 defeat of Manchester United at Highbury followed the loss to Derby County, a Platt header winning it for the Gunners, but a slight wobble had them 13 points behind leaders Manchester United by the end of December. However, this free-scoring, swift-passing and defensively watertight Arsenal side did not lose a game from then on.

With three games remaining, Arsenal met Everton at Highbury on 3 May, with Arsenal knowing that, if they won, they were League champions. First, Slaven Bilic headed into his own net. Second, Overmars made it 2-0 midway through the first half. Third, the little Dutchman ran from the centre circle for 3-0. Fourth, and most gloriously, Arsenal's indomitable captain Tony Adams ran upfield, received a lovely chip from Bould, chested the ball down and thundered a left-foot volley into Everton's net at the North Bank.

Adams stood there beaming, his arms raised high, and he saluted his delirious supporters. 'It was a beautiful moment,' said Tony, holding the League trophy.

There remained the tantalising prospect of the Double coming to Highbury for the second time in Arsenal's history. In early March, Anelka had scored the equaliser in the 1-1 draw with West Ham in the FA Cup quarter-final. The replay took place at Upton Park on 17 March, and Anelka again scored. Bergkamp was sent off with an hour of the match still to play, and the ten-man side resisted the Hammers until Hartson equalised in the dying minutes. Arsenal squeezed through 4-3 on penalties.

In the semi-final, Wreh's goal against Wolves eased Arsenal's route to the Final against Newcastle United. The Geordies were easily overcome by the Gunners, Overmars and, again, Anelka doing the scoring damage. Arsenal had done the Double again, and Wenger celebrated only his second year as manager.

Ian Wright showers the fans at Highbury with champagne after defeating Everton to seal Arsenal's first Premier League title. *Colorsport*

87

What can follow the Double?

There was much more to come from this completely revitalised football team, but there was still work to be done.

The following season saw Wright depart to West Ham and Platt's retirement. In came Swedish midfield dynamo Freddie Ljungberg and Argentine defender Nelson Vivas. After the Double, Arsenal took a while to settle down but, after their near-reserve side was dispatched 5-0 by Chelsea from the League Cup, and they'd been overwhelmed and eliminated by Dynamo Kiev in the Champions League, they were back in form in December. The arrival from AC Milan of gangling Nigerian forward Nwankwo Kanu, a young player with astonishing ball control, undoubtedly helped to spark the revival.

88

'Leave the ball, Kanu'

In the fifth round of the FA Cup against Sheffield United at Highbury, and time running out with the score 1-1, a Sheffield player went down with cramp. He was tended to, and Parlour sportingly threw the ball back towards United, as they had deliberately kicked it into touch. But Kanu, on as a sub in his first game, intercepted and crossed for Overmars, who scored.

United manager Steve Bruce was apoplectic and threatened to withdraw his players from the pitch. Wenger, from the kindness of his heart, offered Bruce a replay but when the replay was mooted to take place in Sheffield, he declined, stating, 'We are sporting but not stupid.' Kanu was much embarrassed by all this, saying, 'I just made a mistake.'

The replay occurred ten days later at Highbury, and Arsenal won 2-1, as they probably would have done in the first place. This little drama made little difference to the FA Cup destination as, after a semi-final replay against Manchester United and a solo Giggs goal, Arsenal were out of the competition.

Arsenal were also pipped at the post in the Premier League by Manchester United. On the final day of the season, Arsenal had to beat Villa (yes) and Spurs had to beat United (no), so Arsenal were second, one point behind United.

89

A brief absence of silverware

This season, 1999/2000, it was again a question of close but not close enough.

Off went Hughes, Boa Morte and Bould (and with him the end of the Famous Five). Anelka moved to Real Madrid for £24 million, realising a profit to Arsenal of £23.5 million and leading Bob Wilson to suggest that, given the financial reconstruction of London Colney, it should be renamed the Nicolas Anelka Training Centre. Defender Silvinho and Croatian centre-forward Davor Suker came to Highbury, as did a 21-year-old winger from Juventus, Thierry Henry.

In the League, Arsenal suffered an October 2-1 defeat by West Ham (Vieira sent off for the fourth time in his Arsenal career) and a November 2-1 defeat by Spurs (their first win over Arsenal for four years). These were balanced in October when losing 2-0 at Chelsea, before a magnificent Kanu hat-trick in the last 15 minutes brought a 3-2 win, as well as a 4-1 January dismissal of Sunderland.

Arsenal were now level with Manchester United, although United had three games in hand. The Gunners, having been knocked out of both Cups, each on penalties, and not winning away from home from early December to mid-March, were now aiming at second in the League – which is where they ended (18 points behind Manchester United) – and a consequent place in next season's Champions League.

A brilliant goal by Fiorentina's Gabriel Batistuta sent them out of the Champions League into this season's UEFA Cup. In March at Highbury, Arsenal's 5-1 win over Deportivo de La Coruña was a stunning and unassailable triumph of all the talents. A Parlour hat-trick in Germany saw off Werder Bremen in the quarter-final, and Lens were beaten at home and away in the semi-final.

In the UEFA Cup Final in Copenhagen on 17 May, Arsenal took on Galatasaray, against a backdrop of violent street battles, punch-ups and stabbings between opposing fans. The game was dull and scoreless throughout, and Turkish danger man Gheorghe Hagi was sent off in extra time for punching Adams in the back. Suker and Vieira both missed their penalties, and Arsenal were defeated.

90

Another Double for Gunners?

Still they come and still they go. Outward bound in 2000/01 were Suker and the long-serving Nigel ('Nutty') Winterburn (13 years, 579 appearances), the latter replaced by Silvinho and the fast-emerging, young Ashley Cole. Also, for a total of £32 million, and against the wishes of Wenger, went Overmars and Petit who decided Barcelona and Real Madrid were better options.

Incomers included winger Robert Pires from Marseilles (a replacement for Overmars), defender Lauren from Real Mallorca and tricky centre-forward Sylvain Wiltord (from Bordeaux).

Arsenal were again out of the League Cup, beaten by Ipswich on 1 November and, on the same day, one of the heroes of the first Double, Geordie Armstrong, collapsed and died from a brain haemorrhage, at the age of 56, at London Colney.

Despite Arsenal's 12-game unbeaten League run and their December destructions of Newcastle (5-0) and Leicester (6-1, with Henry claiming a hat-trick), at the end of the year they were eight points behind Manchester United. By the end of February, and in particular after their 6-1 annihilation at Old Trafford – stand-in Stepanov's abysmal defending did not help – they were 16 points behind, and once more they privately ceded the League title. They ended the season in second place, ten points behind United.

In the Champions League, with Pires quickly demonstrating his importance to the side, Arsenal made it through to the second

HOLSTEN
Dream

The great magician, Thierry Henry, in action against Spurs in the 2001 FA Cup semi-final. *Colorsport*

group stage. Although they lost 1-0 to Bayern Munich in the final group game, they again qualified for the next round, the quarter-final in April against Valencia.

On 31 March David Rocastle died from cancer at the age of 33. In what must have been the late 1980s I bumped into 'Rocky' outside the Clock End entrance on Avenell Road (I was then living a ten-minute stroll from the ground), and I asked him for his autograph for my son. He replied 'Sure, hang on', and loped down Avenell Road. Over 15 minutes later he returned with his publicity pic, and he signed it, saying pleasantly 'Is that all right?' and he walked into Highbury. His car could have been as far away as Finsbury Park, and I was struck by his helpful friendliness. He was a good man. On the day of his death, Arsenal played Spurs at Highbury, and the air of sadness was almost palpable during the one-minute silence in his memory, and it was rigidly observed by all in the ground.

The first leg of the Valencia game was at Highbury on 4 April. The Spanish team ran the game but Arsenal scored twice in the second half for a 2-1 win. At the Mestalla two weeks later, a 1-0 win by Valencia was sufficient to put Arsenal out of Europe on away goals.

There only remained the FA Cup Final. On 12 May, Arsenal were dominant over Liverpool throughout. In the second half Ljungberg opened the scoring, but in the last seven minutes little Michael Owen capitalised on clumsy defending by scoring twice. Liverpool won the FA Cup.

It was beginning to appear to some observers that Arsenal lacked the cutting edge and the will to win, and were perpetual runners-up.

91

Arsene knows

Arsene Wenger, however, knew what he was doing. He was aware he lacked a consistent defence and, with the exception of Henry, a goalscorer. But for Wenger and for Arsenal, season 2001/02 was a domestic triumph.

In came left-midfielder Gio van Bronckhorst, young attacker Franny Jeffers (a disappointment) and, most controversially, central defender Sol Campbell on a free contract from, of all clubs, Spurs. In late August, Brazilian midfielder Edu also arrived. Although Vieira was then unhappy about Arsenal's prospects, and said 'I need to move because I want to win more trophies', he signed an improved new contract.

In the Champions League, Arsenal's passage to the second group stage was assured by a 3-1 win over Real Mallorca. The second group – Deportivo, Bayer Leverkusen and Juventus – was a tough one. Juventus succumbed 3-1 at Highbury. Later in the season, Deportivo gave Arsenal fans at Highbury a masterclass in incisive passing and counter-attacking in a 2-0 win, and they were deservedly applauded off the pitch. A 1-0 defeat in Turin was academic, as results elsewhere meant that Arsenal had failed to qualify for the quarter-finals.

Although there was an increasing and worrying injury list at Highbury, this did not appear to be affecting the results. A 2-1 defeat of Chelsea on Boxing Day saw them at the top of the table, and by now they were playing some stunning football. The goal of the season was in mid-March at Newcastle in the 2-0 win, when Bergkamp flicked the ball past the defender, spun around him and then tapped the ball past the mystified keeper. It was ball control of the highest class.

Off the pitch, Wenger signed a four-year extension to his contract. Also, Islington Council had granted permission for the construction of a 60,000-capacity stadium at Ashburton Grove, a space very close to Highbury. It was all looking very promising for Arsenal.

By the end of April, four straight League wins had the Gunners five points clear, and they only had to draw their penultimate game at Old Trafford to win the title. 'We want to do it at Old Trafford', said Wenger.

On 4 May, Arsenal had achieved the first part of the Double. They had beaten Chelsea 2-0 in the FA Cup Final, thanks to a superb 25-yard curler in the 70th minute from Parlour and another curved shot ten minutes later from Ljungberg from the edge of the box. By 'do it', Wenger was referring to his second Double.

Arsenal achieved their aim on 8 May, and it was indeed at Old Trafford. With their strength of character and focused determination, they held their own against United, and Wiltord scored just after half-time for the only goal of the game. It had been their most crucial match since 1989 against Liverpool, and they had achieved another Double (Arsenal's third) with the style and confidence they had shown throughout this exhausting but profoundly satisfying campaign.

Right: Lee Dixon, Thierry Henry and Ashley Cole lead the celebrations after claiming the 2001/02 Premier League title. *Colorsport*

Dreamcast
BARCLAYCARD

92

The Invincibles

Stemming from the Latin for 'unconquerable', 'Invicta' was the name of the ground Royal Arsenal briefly occupied in the late 19th century. Over a century later, 'Invincible' was again applied to Arsenal as they dominated English league football during season 2003/04.

Talking to the *Sunday Mirror* in August 2003, Arsene Wenger said: 'Nobody will finish above us in the league. It wouldn't surprise me if we were to go unbeaten for the rest of the season.' Although this claim aroused reactions ranging from scepticism to mild derision, and although Preston North End had achieved it (with a smaller league) in 1888/89, Wenger's prediction was again absolutely right.

In 2003/04, Arsenal achieved the remarkable run of 26 wins, 12 draws and no losses in the entire season. The previous season they battled with Manchester United and ended the campaign in second place, a 3-2 defeat at Highbury by Leeds terminating their title aspirations. However, they then became the first team since Spurs in 1982 to win the FA Cup two years in succession.

This season – 2003/04 – not only did Arsenal win the League with a draw at Tottenham but also there were five games yet to play. They won the title by an uncatchable 11 points ahead of Chelsea.

The Invincible season was very much a team effort by a young side, with only two members of the 1998 Double-winning side –

Bergkamp and Vieira – still available. Adams and Dixon had retired in 2002, and Seaman had moved to Manchester City in 2003.

In goal was the often irascible Jens Lehmann. In front of him were Gael Clichy as left-back, with Ashley Cole now established on the right flank, and the centre of defence controlled by Kolo Toure and Sol Campbell. The central midfielders were Gilberto Silva and Vieira, and their wing partners were Pires and Ljungberg. Up front hunted the lethal pairing of Bergkamp and Henry. Others – such as Edu, Kanu and Wiltord – more than adequately filled positions when required, and later in the season the team was joined by young Spanish winger Jose Antonio Reyes. It was an attacking side, which was 4-4-2 or 4-4-1-1 (Wenger's preferred formations) but there were constant switches of position, with the speedy full backs frequently moving forward on the counter-attack.

In fact, the undefeated run began with the penultimate game of the previous season (a 6-1 trouncing of Southampton) and continued into the opening nine matches of 2004/05. In total, this Gunners side were unbeaten for 49 straight League games, an astonishing record. Over the 49-game epic, Henry found the net on 36 occasions and Pires scored 22.

However, some Calvinist once said that all good things must come to an end, and this occurred, of course, at Old Trafford in October 2004, where an undignified foul-fest of a game resulted in a 2-0 defeat by Manchester United and brought a halt to the glorious proceedings. Although Arsenal were knocked out of the other competitions that 2003/04 season, winning the League with such style and panache more than compensated for missing out on these.

Inevitably, the end of the run had a negative, dispiriting impact on the players but they soon perked up. (Interestingly, on

The Invincibles. *Getty Images*

2003

Arsenal
BARCLAYCARD
2004

14 February 2005 Arsenal beat Crystal Palace 5-1 at Highbury and, with Campbell and Cole both injured, Wenger had picked a team which did not contain a single English player. Naturally, the more chauvinist newspapers took this as an insult to English youth, with predictable condemnations.) By the close of 2004/05 they were second in the League, 12 points behind a resurgent Chelsea. They were also knocked out by Bayern Munich in the second round of the Champions League. However, they did win their third FA Cup Final in four years, beating Manchester United on penalties.

93

Last season at Highbury

Over the summer of 2005 Vieira joined Juventus. Missing his dominant presence, Arsenal encountered a spell of poor away form and hovered around mid-table, but they won their last three games to finish in fourth place, in the process edging Spurs into fifth.

Arsenal's final game at Highbury took place on 7 May 2006. It was generally agreed that the 38,500 capacity at Highbury had become too small, and a new stadium – with room for 60,000 – was now completed and awaiting season 2006/07. Highbury had been Arsenal's home for almost a century, but there had been little alternative. Despite the sadness, there was a festive air as Arsenal won the game against Wigan Athletic 4-2, Henry scoring a hat-trick and Pires scoring the other.

Ten days after the Wigan game, Arsenal met Barcelona in the Champions League Final. The Gunners were unbeaten in the group stage, with Henry's two goals against Sparta Prague bringing him the mantle of the club's all-time top goalscorer.

On their way to the Final, they became the first English club to defeat Real Madrid at the Bernabeu, and they drew at home. Juventus were next, and were defeated 2-0 at home and drew 0-0 in Turin. Then a Kolo Toure penalty in Spain against Villarreal gave Arsenal a 1-0 advantage, and a last-minute penalty save by Lehmann at home saw Arsenal through to their first Champions League Final.

On 17 May, they met Barcelona in the Final at the Parc des Princes. In the 18th minute Lehmann was sent off for a professional foul. Wenger's decision to replace him with reserve keeper Manuel Almunia meant the withdrawal of a player, in this case an unhappy Pires. Campbell scored for the ten men with a first-half header, and Arsenal defended stoutly, only to concede two late goals. Barcelona won 2-1.

94

Early years at the Emirates

Until 2006 Ashburton Grove was 17 acres of land in north London, which contained a waste transfer station and various small businesses, the area being owned by Islington Council. Today, it is the Emirates Stadium, and is the new home of Arsenal. Construction work began in January 2002, and the stadium was completed in the early summer of 2006, in time for its first match: Dennis Bergkamp's testimonial against Ajax on 22 July.

The Emirates is a typical modern football stadium, containing seats for 60,500 spectators, lacking the homely familiarity of Highbury but offering a range of eating, drinking and shopping outlets which were rare indeed at the old stadium. As well as being able to accommodate 20,000 more people, the pitch is bigger (113x76m as against 105x70m), although further away from the fans. It is located only a few hundred yards from Highbury (when exiting Arsenal station on the Piccadilly Line, turn right instead of left). The Emirates takes a while in which to feel comfortable, but one soon gets used to it.

The first competitive match in the Emirates was a 1-1 draw with Aston Villa on 19 August. That first season witnessed the departure of several senior players, including Campbell, Cole (in part-exchange for William Gallas), Ljungberg, Lauren, Pires and, in 2007, Henry. Cesc Fabregas, a brilliant young midfielder and by then a regular in the team, commented on Henry that 'he was a great player but it was not easy to play alongside him', his implication perhaps being that this was now a younger, different team but an equally talented one: just watch us.

However, despite young Fabregas' admirable, occasionally breath-taking skills and his creative importance to his team – a description which also applies to several of his fellow players – Arsenal did not win a major trophy between the Emirates move and 2013/14, a period referred to as 'The Trophy Drought'.

The first season at the Emirates – 2006/07 – was one of transition and of adjusting to the new environment and to departing and incoming players, the latter including 17-year-old winger Theo Walcott. Arsenal did reach the League Cup Final, but they were beaten 2-1 by Chelsea, and they were in fourth place at season's end.

95

Gunners knock out AC Milan

AC Milan, one of Europe's great clubs, had won the Champions League in 2007/08, the seventh time in their history they had claimed the European Cup/Champions League title. Among their team of renowned footballers was Kaka, the reigning World Player of the Year.

In February 2008 Arsenal, who had fought their way through the group stage to the last 16 teams in the tournament, played Milan at the Emirates and secured a 0-0 draw. On 5 March, the two sides met for the second leg in Milan at the daunting San Siro stadium. Courtesy of late goals from Fabregas and Emmanuel Adebayor, Arsenal eliminated Milan 2-0, and they became the first English side to beat Milan at the Italian club's home ground.

After the match, a delighted Wenger praised his players, saying: 'It was a perfectly executed performance ... I'm very proud of my team.' Arsenal were themselves defeated by Liverpool in the subsequent quarter-final, but they could be proud of their San Siro achievement.

Despite the defensive efforts of Alex Song, Gael Clichy and William Gallas, the growing influence of 20-year-old Fabregas, and the attacking flair of Robin Van Persie and Adebayor, Arsenal were fourth in 2008/09.

Inconsistency has often been identified with Arsenal, but there now also appeared to be a lack of empathy and little sense of their mutual dependency as a team, perhaps indicated by the constant coming and going of players, and linked to the team's overall inexperience. In the summer of 2009, Adebayor and Toure departed. With Fabregas having assumed the captaincy from an increasingly erratic William Gallas in 2009/10, a major injury to Welsh midfield star Aaron Ramsey disrupted the season. Arsenal also reached the quarter-final of the Champions League but were beaten 6-3 on aggregate by Barcelona, Messi scoring four in the second game at the Nou Camp. Nevertheless, Arsenal were third in the League, their 15th successive top-five placing.

From around 2010, there was a feeling among a growing number of supporters that it was time for Wenger to leave, and they expressed this vociferously. Attendances, too, were declining at the Emirates. However, Wenger, who considered his work to be incomplete, was offered and signed a new four-year contract. Season 2010/11 saw Arsenal lose 2-1 to Birmingham City in the League Cup Final and defeated by Manchester United in the FA Cup, but their more impressive League form kept them at fourth spot in the Premiership.

These barren years in their new stadium played their part in persuading three of the club's major playing assets – Cesc Fabregas, Gael Clichy and Samir Nasri – to leave over the summer. Season 2011/12 began with a deeply humiliating 8-2 destruction by Manchester United at Old Trafford, Arsenal's biggest loss since 1927. Calls were now increasingly being heard for Wenger's sacking. Van Persie, the club's leading scorer for the last two years (30 League goals the previous season), left at the beginning of 2012/13, as did Alex Song.

In came strikers Olivier Giroud and Lukas Podolski and attacking midfielder/winger Santi Cazorla to team up with the earlier signings of Mikel Arteta and Per Mertesacker, but Arsenal were again eliminated from the cups and the Champions League, although they remained in the League top five.

Cesc Fabregas strikes against Chelsea. *Getty Images*

96

Three trophies in four years

Finally, in the following season of 2013/14 Arsenal won their first trophy since leaving Highbury: the FA Cup. They also won it the following year and, two seasons later, they repeated the trick. Three FA Cups in four seasons is not bad going, and it does suggest a return to a greater consistency and team coherence.

The first trophy was in 2014 against Hull City, who were 2-0 ahead as early as the eighth minute but who were eventually beaten 3-2 in extra time. Midfield playmaker Mesut Ozil also joined from Real Madrid. The second FA Cup, in 2015, was a more emphatic 4-0 defeat of Aston Villa. Also in that season of 2014/15 a new striker, Alexis Sanchez arrived, and young wing-back Hector Bellerin entered the senior team.

The third FA Cup Final took place in 2017, with Chelsea the opponents. This was a more entertaining football spectacle than the previous two Finals, and Arsenal secured the trophy for a record 13th time with a header from Aaron Ramsey and a final score of 2-1. The previous season had seen more newcomers – midfielder Granit Xhaka and centre-back Shkodran Mustafi, and Sanchez was already making his impact in 2016/17 with 24 goals to his credit – but they ended fifth in the League.

However, Arsenal showed little real improvement in the European cups or in the Premiership during this period. Although (or perhaps because) two more strikers, Alexandre Lacazette and

Pierre-Emerick Aubameyang – record signings both – were now available, Sanchez moved to Manchester United. At the end of the 2017/18 season, Arsenal were beaten by Forest in the FA Cup third round and finished sixth in the League.

It was time for the Arsenal board of directors to have an urgent word or two with Wenger concerning the manager's future.

Alexis Sanchez in action against Chelsea at Wembley in the 2017 FA Cup Final. *Colorsport*

97

Au revoir, Arsene

On 20 April 2018, Wenger announced that he would be leaving Arsenal at the end of the 2017/18 season. On his final game in charge – a 5-0 win over Burnley – Wenger received a standing ovation from his grateful supporters, and well did he deserve this farewell mark of respect. He is a man who can be ranked alongside the legendary Herbert Chapman as one of the greatest Arsenal managers.

As well as his many personal awards and achievements, in his 22 years as manager Wenger steered Arsenal to three Premier League titles (two of which were Doubles), seven FA Cups and a Champions League Final. He also guided the club to its appearance in the Champions League for 19 successive seasons, which was then a European record surpassed only by Real Madrid.

However, in his autobiography Wenger states: 'My departure from Arsenal was a very tough, very painful moment.' He had been particularly upset in 2007 by the rather acrimonious departure from the Arsenal board of his close friend and confidant David Dein. Dein was a genuine football man, who visited the players in their post-match dressing room, was one of the main figures in the creation of the Premier League, was the man who oversaw the creation of the new North Bank stand, and much more. In my limited personal experience of Dein, in a book-publishing capacity, I found him friendly and helpful, and he seemed to be admired and respected by his colleagues.

An instance, which well illustrates Dein's prescience and determination, comes from a meeting Dein had in 1983 with the then-chairman of Arsenal, Peter Hill-Wood. Dein offered him £292,000 for a 16.6% shareholding in the club, and Hill-Wood accepted the deal, but he also said that the offer was 'crazy . . . to all intents and purposes, it's dead money'. Dein's shareholding and board status varied over the years, but in 2007 he sold his 14.6% final share in Arsenal to Alisher Usmanov for around £75 million. Crazy? I think not.

Dein had long been a powerful and supportive advocate of Wenger. Indeed, he was the man who had brought the Frenchman – as well as such players as Bergkamp and Wright – to the club. It is little surprise that Wenger had found Dein's departure to have been one of the 'painful' moments which the ex-manager mentions in his book.

However, Wenger had said, when announcing his imminent departure, that 'it is time for change at the club'. And so, the Wenger era came to an end.

98

Zorte on*, Unai

** (Basque for 'Good Luck')*

On Wenger's departure, ex-player (and underwear model advertising star) Freddie Ljungberg assumed, on an interim basis, the managerial role.

This lasted only until 23 May 2018 with the appointment of Unai Emery as 'head coach' on a two-year contract. Emery's job title was the first time that this had been used at Arsenal, and perhaps reflects the influence of US multi-millionaire Stan Kroenke who, by August that year, assumed full control of Arsenal.

Basque-born Emery had enjoyed a successful managerial career at Valencia and then Sevilla where, under his leadership, they became the first, and only club to date, to win the UEFA Cup / Europa League three years in succession (2014 to 2016). When Arsenal came calling, Emery was in charge at PSG. Like Wenger, he was something of an unknown quantity in England.

In preparation for season 2018/19, he acquired new players. These included German keeper Bernd Leno, Greek centre-back Sokratis, Uruguayan midfield playmaker Lucas Torreira and French teenage midfielder Matteo Guendouzi: a grouping which further underlined the international status of the Arsenal first team. They lost their first two games of the season, but then set off on a 22-game unbeaten streak in all competitions, a feat unseen at Arsenal since 1987. Southampton brought this to a halt in mid-December.

Results then began to unravel. Arsenal were defeated by Spurs in the League Cup, defeated at home by Liverpool and Chelsea, and kicked out of the FA Cup by Manchester United, but they managed fifth place in the League that season. However, in their last game – the Europa League Final on 29 May in Azerbaijan – Arsenal were humbled 4-1 by Chelsea.

For the following season, he brought in teenage Brazilian forward Gabriel Martinelli, winger and club record signing Pepe, and midfielder Dani Ceballos (on loan). For defence, he prised the excellent young left-back Kieran Tierney from Celtic, as well as the occasionally unpredictable but much-experienced centre-back David Luiz from Chelsea. He also allowed several other players – for instance, Ramsey, Koscielny and Monreal – to depart the club.

However, although Arsenal started well in 2019/20, their form then began to decline. After a run of defeats and poor performances, the last being a 1-2 defeat by Eintracht Frankfurt, on 29 November 2019 Emery was sacked by Arsenal.

One could argue that Emery was not given sufficient time to develop the team he wanted and, in the modern game, 17 months does seem a rather brief period in which to judge such an undertaking. One could also defend Arsenal's abrupt decision by the fact that virtually all of Emery's prior managerial successes, in particular with Valencia and Sevilla, were with Spanish clubs, and that he was unaccustomed to the culture of Premiership football.

Indeed, and this may sound overly chauvinistic but, internationally diverse though the Arsenal players were, the language of football in England is, well, English. Wenger spoke six languages, and he was fluent in English. When I listened to TV interviews with Emery, he seemed to have a halting, even distant relationship with the required native tongue, and this may have hindered his discussions with some of the players and staff at Arsenal. However, whatever the reason: agur. (*Basque for 'goodbye'.*)

99

An ex-captain returns

Within one month of Emery's departure, another Basque-born manager – but one rather more Anglified than Emery – was appointed as Arsenal's manager.

On 20 December 2019 Mikel Arteta, who played for the Highbury club between 2011 and 2016 and was captain for his final two years, was created head coach on a three-and-a-half-year contract. As a player, Arteta had signed as a junior with Barcelona. He then moved to Rangers, Real Sociedad and Everton as a midfielder before joining Arsenal. After retiring from playing in 2016, he was appointed assistant coach at Manchester City under Pep Guardiola.

At the end of Arteta's first managerial season at Arsenal, the club finished in eighth place in the League – Arsenal's lowest finish since 1994/95 – but he cannot be entirely blamed for this. However, his team won the 2020 FA Cup, coming from behind and defeating Chelsea 2-1 with two goals from Aubameyang. Arteta said of Aubameyang, 'I want to build the squad around him' (the striker had also scored twice in the semi-final against Manchester City).

Over the summer of 2020, Arteta's designation of 'head coach' was changed to 'manager', obviously signifying approval from above of his tactics.

100

'Arsenal fall short . . .'

Despite his elevation, however, Arteta and Arsenal in 2020/21 suffered their worst season for a good many years, as the above quotation from an early-May 2022 edition of the *Guardian* indicates.

Not only were Arsenal knocked out of both domestic cups, but they also failed to secure a place in European football for the following season, for the first time in 25 years. Although the season's arrivals included such potentially high-quality players as winger Willian, central midfielder Thomas Partey, centre-back Gabriel, midfielder Martin Odegaard and others, Arsenal had, by their standards, endured a fairly dismal season. It was mainly due to the younger players, particularly Tierney, Smith-Rowe and Saka, that even their lowly position was maintained.

As I write, with the season now over, they finished eighth in the League and were knocked out of the penultimate stage in Europe. I watched both legs of the Europa League semi-final, when Arsenal were beaten 2-1 away by Villarreal and could only manage a 0-0 draw at the Emirates. In both games, Arsenal lacked cohesion and purpose, and they were deservedly defeated. The obvious irony is that the Spanish club are coached by the very man, Unai Emery, who was sacked to make way for Arteta. Emery out-thought and out-guessed Arteta, and his team out-played the Gunners.

I write these words with a heavy heart, as I would have much preferred to conclude this book with an image of Arteta holding up the trophy, but to brush over the current reality would be untruthful and unhelpful. Nevertheless, it is quite conceivable that this proud and determined club could win the Champions League in the near future. Who can tell with Arsenal?

As an Arsenal supporter for well over 45 years, I have lived with the extremes of both joy and despair. This renowned club will soon be back among the elite of English and European football, as has been proven by its unparalleled ability to overcome near-disaster and to embrace deserved triumph throughout its fascinating roller-coaster history.

As the North Bank supporters used to chant:

'Ooo, ooo, ooo to be
Ooo to be a Gooner'

It'll take a lot more than one difficult season – and Arsenal have had plenty of these – to diminish the loyalty of these Gooners and, indeed, of all Arsenal supporters worldwide. As validation of the strength of their commitment to the club, one need only read (in 101 over the page) the outrage expressed by fans at the recently revealed proposal for a European Super League.

101

'Legacy Fans 1, Billionaires 0'

In mid-April 2021, six of the leading wealthy clubs in England announced that they, along with four similar clubs in Europe, were seriously discussing the establishment of what they described as a European Super League. These clubs were Manchester United, Manchester City, Liverpool, Chelsea, Tottenham Hotspur and, unfortunately, Arsenal.

This proposed League would be by invitation, there would be no relegation or promotion or risk and reward (the basis of the existing league systems), and they would be owned by mega-rich non-English individuals or concerns. The clubs appeared to believe that fans, players and all who love the game are a declining revenue source, and that the clubs' money streams would be significantly improved by the implementation of this proposed new elite league. Never mind the long history and traditions of football: the league would be a financial windfall to these new owners.

The reaction to this proposal was one of furious intensity, the like of which I have rarely, if ever, encountered in the English game. Many supporters had complained about, for instance, the changing structures of the Champions League and the arrival of the Premier League, but they accepted them. However, this new league aroused acute anger and heated demonstrations against these owners' attempts to destroy the basis of the fans' national game. For instance, several thousand Arsenal fans protested outside the Emirates before the 23 April game against Everton, many carrying placards stating 'Kroenkes Out' and 'Fan ownership now'. There were many more such protests. Strong objections to the Super League even came from the British government.

As a result of the furore, several club owners – including the Kroenke family – publicly apologised, realising they had seriously miscalculated the depth of the emotions generated by English club football. The Super League plans, we are assured, have now been shelved. There will no doubt be plans to resuscitate them, but they are at present off the owners' agendas.

I sincerely hope that attending matches, talking to fans and reading books, such as this one, will go some way to revealing to club owners the strong, enduring relationship which many people have with the game of football.

POLARIS
PUBLISHING